About the author

William Cull was an apprentice coach builder from Sanford, Victoria, who enlisted in the AIF in May 1915. He saw active service as an infantry officer on Gallipoli and the Western Front where he was severely wounded and taken prisoner during the 6th Brigade's attack on Malt Trench near Warlencourt in February 1917. He spent eleven months in captivity in Germany before being transferred to Switzerland in January 1918. He died in Melbourne in 1939.

About the editor

Aaron Pegram is a historian at the Australian War Memorial and the Managing Editor of the Memorial's magazine *Wartime*. A Charles Sturt University history graduate, he is currently writing a PhD thesis on the 3,861 Australian troops taken prisoner by the German Army on the Western Front.

BOTH SIDES OF
THE WIRE

BOTH SIDES OF
THE WIRE

The memoir of an Australian officer captured
during the Great War

WILLIAM CULL

EDITED BY AARON PEGRAM

ALLEN&UNWIN

First published in 2011
Originally published in 1919 as *At All Costs*

Allen & Unwin
Sydney, Melbourne, Auckland, London

83 Alexander Street
Crows Nest NSW 2065
Australia
Phone: (61 2) 8425 0100
Fax: (61 2) 9906 2218
Email: info@allenandunwin.com
Web: www.allenandunwin.com

Cataloguing-in-Publication details are available
from the National Library of Australia
www.trove.nla.gov.au

ISBN 978 1 74237 616 5

Maps by Keith Mitchell
Typeset in 12.5/16.5 pt Perpetua by Post Pre-press Group, Australia
Printed and bound in Australia by Griffin Press

Page viii: Captain William Ambrose Cull, 22nd Battalion, in London
after thirteen months as a prisoner of war in German captivity.
Reproduced from *At All Costs*, 1919.

10 9 8 7 6 5 4 3 2 1

Contents

W. AMBROSE CULL
(Captain Late A.I.F.)

Introduction

Captain William Ambrose Cull, 22nd Battalion, Australian Imperial Force (AIF), was taken prisoner on the Western Front early on the morning of 26 February 1917. A veteran of the Gallipoli campaign and the fighting at Pozières on the Somme, Cull was seriously wounded in the hip by fragments of a German hand grenade as he led his company during a brigade attack on Malt Trench—a formidable German stronghold just outside of the French village of Le Barque, which was well protected by thick belts of barbed wire, machine guns, and a garrison of well-trained and experienced German troops.

It was vital for attacks like these to be made with the assistance of large amounts of artillery that would cut paths through the wire and keep the Germans in their dugouts instead of at their machine guns, but this attack had no such support. Elsewhere, the Germans had withdrawn from their positions—so tenaciously held throughout the Battle of the Somme and the depressing winter that followed—so that they could stand and fight the Allied armies along the Hindenburg Line many miles to the east. British and Dominion troops, including the Australians, followed in their wake, some re-establishing contact with determined German machine-gunners standing to fight a rearguard action. But Malt Trench was believed by Australian commanders to be lightly held and could easily be taken by the advancing infantry. Because the rest of the Allied front was following up on the German withdrawal, the commanders were eager that the attack be made and the objective secured. Cull headed out into No Man's Land to patrol the German wire the night before the attack, but found the German bastion at Malt Trench to be held by a powerful and determined enemy that was willing to stand their ground. He protested to his commanders, telling them how futile such an attack would be, but in reply was told curtly that 'not a shell' would be fired and that 'the attack must be launched at all costs.'

His objections ignored, Cull led his men within sixty yards of the uncut enemy wire before they were met by a wall of German rifle and machine-gun fire. Images of soldiers being hung up on barbed wire and slaughtered by machine guns is probably one of the most pervasive and exaggerated stereotypes of trench fighting during the First World War, but without the firepower to beat down the German wires it was the reality that faced Cull and his men that night in their attack on Malt Trench. Illuminated by German flares, Cull tells us that in the face of the murderous machine-gun fire, his 'doomed but dauntless men' tore at the German wire 'with bare and bleeding hands' in the effort to press on with the attack.

Cull negotiated the first belt of barbed wire and was making his way through a second when a German hand grenade landed at his feet and exploded, tearing away part of his hip and blowing him out in the open. He was dragged by his men to the safety of a nearby shell hole, but they were unable to bring him back to the Australian positions when they later withdrew. Owing to the loss of blood, Cull drifted in and out of consciousness for hours, but was mortified to wake to the sound of German troops moving about the uncut wire, searching for survivors. For Cull, the sudden realisation that he was going to be taken prisoner was purely mortifying: 'Now that there was no longer any hope of escape, I wished they would come, though what the Battalion would think of me if they knew that I was taken prisoner worried me. The thought was so bitter that for a moment I cared little whether I lived or died.' Cull's worst fears materialised in the form of a German soldier who discovered the wounded and bleeding Australian at the bottom of his shell hole, and brought him into the trenches that Cull and his men had so desperately tried to take.

William Cull thus became one of 4057 Australians taken prisoner during the First World War.[1] I first came across his book, originally titled *At All Costs*, at the beginning of my PhD research on the Australians captured on the Western Front. Charles Bean, the Australian official historian, used Cull's description of the attack on Malt Trench in Volume IV of the *Official History of Australia in the war of 1914–1918*, and Bill Gammage used Cull's letters in the State Library of NSW for his PhD thesis which ultimately became *The Broken Years*— the landmark study of Australians during the First World War. Hundreds of books document the horror that 21,400 Australians suffered in Japanese captivity during the Second World War, but *At All Costs* was one of the very few publications that I could find on the Australians that had been captured a generation before. As it turned out, Cull's was one of just four published accounts written by the 3867 Australians held captive by the Germans, and like the 196 Australians captured by Ottoman Turkey, their account of hardship and anguish was quickly forgotten by a nation deep in mourning. The loss of up to 60,000 Australians on the cliffs of Gallipoli, in the deserts of Sinai-Palestine and Mesopotamia, and in the putrid mud of France and Flanders was a burden simply far too great to bear for such a young nation.

I was immediately struck by how frank and candid Cull's account of the war truly was; not only of his capture and ordeal as a wounded Australian officer in the hands of the Germans, but of his brief service on the Gallipoli peninsular and the gritty reality of trench warfare on the Western Front. Unlike other memoirs I had read by returned servicemen writing in the late 1920s and 1930s, *At All Costs* had a raw sense of immediacy that had not yet had the chance to mellow with the benefit of time. Cull speaks bitterly about his enemy, using the dehumanising labels of 'Hun' and 'Bosche' instead of the affable 'Fritz' of more measured writers. Unlike other authors, Cull writes openly and candidly about the thrill of stalking men in No Man's Land, the psychology of battle, and the personal sense of humiliation felt at becoming a prisoner of war. Most revealing was Cull's description of the nature of raiding and patrolling in the so-called 'quiet sector' near Armentières, known as 'The Nursery', where Australian troops learned the rigours and routine of warfare on the Western Front after their arrival from Egypt in March 1916. Here, the surrender of 'treacherous' Germans was not always accepted, although this grim reality of trench fighting was a subject that few front line memoirists could be frank about. Bean gave several examples of it throughout the *Official History*, but explained that such things were inevitable in close quarters fighting that depended on the 'exercise of primitive instinct' for survival. It was one of the many realities that troops faced on the Western Front, although Cull had the misfortune of learning that the Germans, too, would at times not take prisoners.

At All Costs first appeared in 1919 at a time when governments across the British Empire were concerned about how the vanquished Central Powers had treated its prisoners of war. From 1915 until the end of the war, the British Committee on the treatment by the enemy of British prisoners of war regularly released reports on the conditions Allied prisoners were facing in enemy captivity. These reports were based on interviews from the wounded and sick who had been repatriated to England, escaped prisoners of war, and various forms of correspondence that had been mediated by the neutral countries to and from the German War Ministry. Excerpts were routinely published in the British press, where they proved to be of great propaganda value, but Australians were mortified when reports from occupied France told for the first time how their own troops were faring in the hands of the German Army.

In May 1917, Charles Bean, then the Australian war correspondent, interviewed two men who had been among the 1170 Australians captured during the 4th Division's costly and unsuccessful attack on the Hindenburg Line at Bullecourt on 11 April 1917—the largest group of Australians taken prisoner in a single engagement throughout the entirety of the war. They had escaped from behind German lines, and had brought with them news that the unwounded other-ranks men were being held as 'prisoners of respite' in deliberate violation of the 1907 Hague Convention, and were being used as labourers within the range of Allied artillery fire. Their poor treatment, according to the Germans, was in retaliation of the British Army using captured Germans as labourers behind its front line, and would continue until all German prisoners were removed from within 30 kilometres of the British lines. In reality, however, a German manpower shortage following heavy casualties at Verdun and on the Somme the previous year ensured that the captured Australians remained behind German lines as labourers until as late as November 1917. The escaped men told a tale of woeful neglect, random beatings and lootings, inadequate provisions, and extreme hunger, which only affirmed the image of the German Army as a cruel and merciless enemy. 'They can starve and ill-treat them as much as they like,' Bean thundered in one of his despatches. 'One can only thank Providence that Australians have a long, long memory, and that the Germans may regret for centuries the months when they did their will upon these 1000 men.'[2]

News such as this was fragmentary at its best, so it was only after the war that the full story of the treatment of Australian prisoners emerged from the prison camps of Germany and Ottoman Turkey when men like Cull began to tell their stories. After their repatriation to England, over 2000 Australian prisoners of war gave written statements about the circumstances of their capture and the quality of their treatment in the hands of the enemy. Treatment varied according to rank, the theatre of operations in which a man was captured, the enemy unit that captured him, whether he was wounded or not, whether he remained for long periods of time behind the enemy front line; and when he did eventually make it into the prison camps, the location of that camp within the enemy nation. Australian prisoners experienced extremes at both ends of the spectrum, but unlike the sufferings of Australian prisoners in the Pacific during the Second World War, no unified narrative emerged from the prison camps of the Central Powers. Conditions in Turkey were simply horrible with 60 Australians (30 per cent of Australians taken prisoner by the Turks) dying in captivity, mainly as a result of disease. Conditions in Germany were much better, where 337 of Australian prisoners died (8 per cent of Australians captured by the Germans), almost three quarters of which were from wounds received in battle.[3]

With the notable exception of the deliberate mistreatment of the Australians captured at Bullecourt, Germany overwhelmingly adhered to the rules outlined by the 1907 Hague Convention. As an officer, Cull was given better treatment than the NCO and other-ranks prisoners. Once his wounds had healed sufficiently at the hospital at Bochum, Cull was held in officer camps at Karlsruhe, Freiburg and Heidelberg in southern Germany with other British prisoners where he could draw pay, could at times be given parole (based on the gentleman's agreement that no escape attempts be made), and was never put to work.

Vital for prisoner survival in Germany were the regular consignments of mail and food parcels from the Red Cross Society, which all Australian prisoners in Germany were able to live off rather than the inadequate camp provisions.

Australian prisoners in Turkey also received food parcels from the Red Cross, but the unreliable supply lines across the Austro-Hungarian Empire and the isolated regions of the Turkish prison camps made distributing welfare to prisoners extremely difficult.

In spite of the better conditions Australian prisoners experienced in Germany, selected statements that described the worst of the treatment at the hands of the German people were published in 1919 by the Department of Defence, under the title *How the Germans treated Australian prisoners of war*. With the Treaty of Versailles yet to be signed, the publication served as an indictment for defeated Germany to pay for its outrages committed against prisoners of war. The other prisoner of war memoirs were published in Australia at this time, but the observation that the vast majority of Australians survived captivity and the war seems to be one made with the benefit of hindsight rather than the view shared at the time.

Unlike the other memoirs written by returned Australian servicemen, *At All Costs* gave a unique perspective of the burden of war felt by the people on the other side of the wire. In 1914 the British imposed a naval blockade of Germany which produced critical shortages in basic areas such as fertilisers, fats and other basic commodities. International trade collapsed, and Germany lost millions in finance and commerce. The armaments industry was sufficiently controlled by the state to continue production until the end of the war, but agriculture was not so well organised and was strained by a massive army with a voracious appetite as well as the needs of millions of people at home. As in all countries, Germany was forced to impose wartime rationing, but a haphazard attempt by the state to fix pricing at the point of production, not at the point of sale, encouraged producers to withdraw from the market. This caused massive inflation of essential food items such as milk, vegetables and fruit. A potato shortage was attributed to the enormous consumption of fodder required by stock, and millions of pigs were slaughtered in the great *Schweindemord* of 1915. No pigs meant little fertiliser, which worsened existing problems caused by the failed crops of 1914–1915 and the 'turnip winter' of 1916–1917. Meat became scarce. Conditions on the home front deteriorated as the war dragged on, and by the time the first Australian prisoners had arrived in Germany in mid-1916, the German population had long been feeling the effects of the war in the pits of their stomachs. But with regular consignments of food parcels sent to them by the Red Cross in London, Australian prisoners were completely self-sufficient from the Germans' meagre ration of turnips, *Kriegsbrot* and *ersatz* coffee, and by late 1917, they were easily among the best-fed people in the country.

Cull's story is, therefore, a very different account of the First World War than many Australians are familiar with. It is not a story of courage and heroism, because Cull certainly did not see it in such a way, but rather a story of the adversity, perseverance, tragedy and resentment of a young Australian who spent thirteen months as a prisoner of war in Germany. Cull's story is both powerful and evocative, and contributes to our greater understanding of the sacrifice made by Australians during the First World War.

In *Both Sides of the Wire* I have kept Cull's story very much as it appeared in its original published form from 1919, with the notable exceptions of the introduction, endnotes, epilogue and title. All mistakes appearing in these sections are none other but my own. The notes have been included in this edition to set Cull's story within the broader experience of captivity during the First World War and to convey to the reader that the war for William Cull continued many years after his repatriation to Australia. Where possible I have corrected the spelling of locations and place names in Egypt, France and Germany, and have taken the liberty of including the ranks, Christian names and units of people influential in Cull's story for wider interest.

Aaron Pegram

6th Brigade attack, 25 February 1917

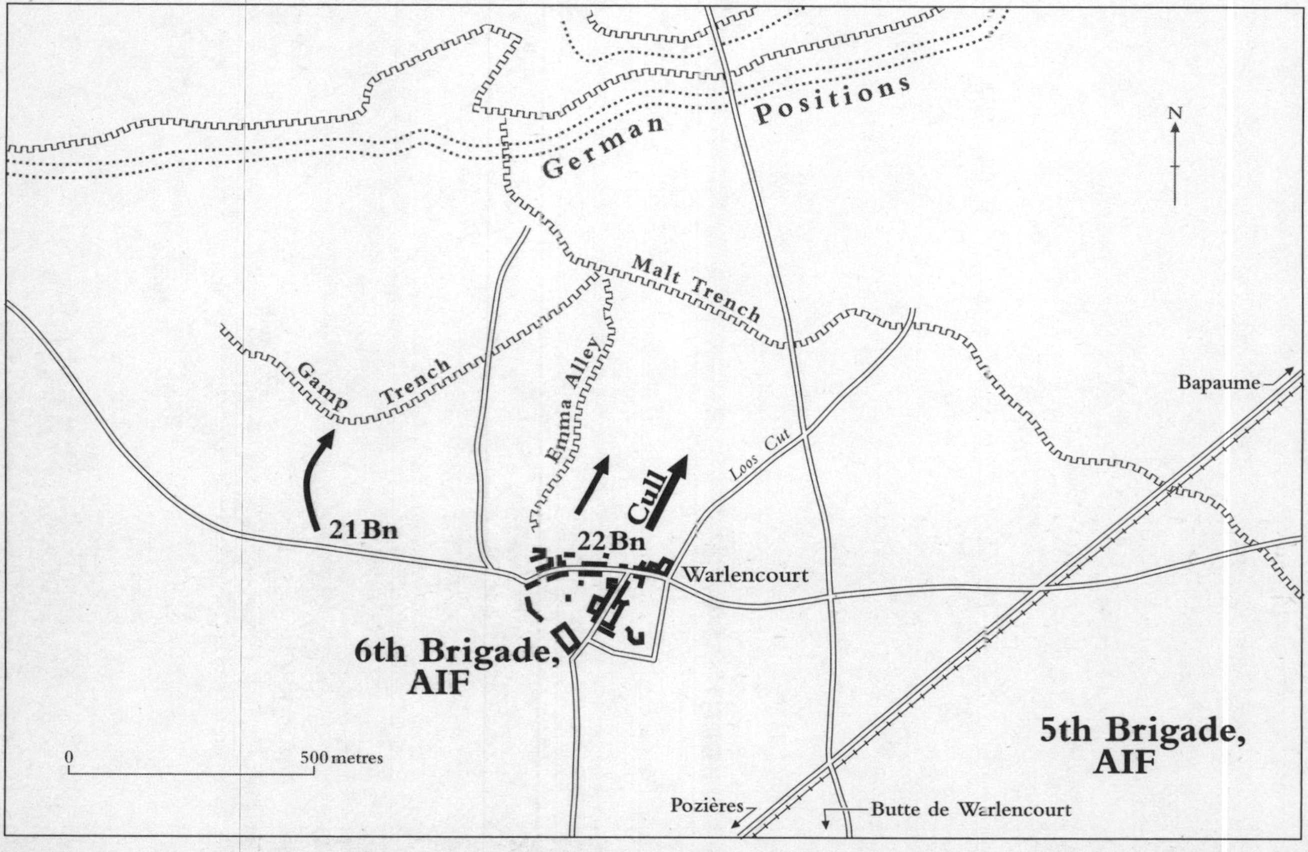

N

Bapaume

German Positions

Malt Trench

Emma Alley

Loos Cut

Cut

22 Bn

Gamp Trench

21 Bn

Warlencourt

Butte de Warlencourt

Pozières

5th Brigade, AIF

6th Brigade, AIF

0   500 metres

Chapter 1

Egypt and Gallipoli

The story of the Australian training camps in Egypt, the dramatic assault upon the Turkish cliff trenches of Gallipoli, where so many of our men had their baptism of fire, where many sleep in silent company, has been often told, so it is necessary only to offer a few personal impressions and experiences of that campaign.

Prior to the war I held a commission in the citizen military forces, but that, apparently, was not considered a vital recommendation for war service, because it was only on the twelfth application and after repeated offers of service in any capacity that I was finally accepted and sent to Duntroon for the special course. In any case the age limit of twenty-one years—soon afterwards extended to twenty-three—for commissions would have proved a barrier to holding commission rank at the age of twenty with the AIF, though not with the Imperial Forces, for, in despair of seeing war service at home, I had applied to the War Office, and in Egypt later was offered a commission. In the meantime I had passed out of Duntroon as one of five special instructors for Broadmeadows Camp, and once enrolled with the Australians, there was, naturally, no desire for service elsewhere, even though accompanied with that offer of rank which was denied at home.

As a result of many disappointments both before and after enlistment, I missed the heroic landing at Gallipoli, and to an Anzac that much has ever been a matter of regret. Beginning as a Private, I had gained my Sergeant's stripes when eventually I got away with the 6th Brigade under Lieutenant Colonel George Morton, commanding officer of the 23rd Battalion, who had been my battalion commander in home soldiering with the 71st City of Ballarat Regiment. Both on Gallipoli and in France it was my good fortune to serve under officers identified with the Ballarat district.

Egypt had been called the land of sun, sin, sorrow and sore eyes. Its temperatures are as high as its morals are unquestionably low, and Cairo is qualified in both ways to be its capital. One had to be very young indeed, very unobservant, not to realise the pity that Australian troops were ever landed there at all, even though it paved the way to Gallipoli and the name and fame of Anzac. It was in one sense dramatically picturesque that it should have fallen to the lot of the youngest nation amongst the Allies to sojourn in Egypt and campaign in Palestine—two of the cradles of the world. Their immemorial ruins were fingerposts pointing us always back to the grey days of antiquity, giving a new meaning to Scripture and history. The pity is that the contrast between past and present should, in its human elements, be so marked. There is nothing inspiring in the Egyptian today. He represents squalor and vice at its worst, and into these centres of decadence were dumped thousands of young Australians, many of whom had just thrown aside their school books, ignorant of the dangers of their surroundings, full of confidence in themselves. Their first knowledge of the outside world might have been gained in much better company and in a cleaner atmosphere. It was especially hard upon lads who were playing the man's game, with very little preparation for it. Apart from the desire for action, no one was sorry to see the last of Egypt.

Our first touch of hostilities on the way to the Turkish coast came with the torpedoing of the *Southland*, our transport being near enough at the time to assist in the rescue of her troops. The death of Colonel Richard Linton, commanding officer of the 6th Brigade, was to me a matter of deep regret, because it was mainly upon his very strong recommendation that I had finally obtained the chance for active service. Even in the Lone Pine trenches, with the zip of sniper bullets always about one's ears, the occasional boom of big artillery, and the very near presence of the unspeakable Turk, it was difficult for one to realise that he had reached the Mecca of his pilgrimage. Even this early in my experience of war and with prying aeroplanes frequently crossing over our lines, I began to realise that the machine could never alter or lower the status of the human scout. The glamour of night work, of creeping and peering through the darkness to get touch of the enemy and some knowledge of his intentions began then to get possession of me. The searching of actual war finds elements and qualities in many forms. Under its grim influence one must discover himself afresh, though the finest find of all is that which he discovers in others, the spirit and full meaning of comradeship, the depths never before plumbed which the grim psychology of battle alone reveals. To have seen the souls and hearts of men laid bare is to know men—the very flower of men—in a new phase, and in that knowledge to be forever exalted.

The duller weeks of Gallipoli, in which both sides hung grimly to their lines, each watching and waiting for the other to lead, passed on with such excitements as an occasional bit of sniping, a constant vigilance in the matter of spies, for in this we were able to teach Abdul little. He took the ventures of it, both in our uniform and his own, and in this proved himself a brave soldier. In all the work of war time, none is more widely misunderstood than that of the military spy. Knowing well that, even on the faintest suspicion, he will be riddled with volleys of awkward questions, trusting wholly to his own mental alertness to survive that ordeal, he goes into enemy lines fully aware that discovery means short shrift and sudden death. Only the soldier can understand and appreciate all the risks of such a duty, the vital importance of success, the inevitable consequences of failure. The civilian scorns him, but the soldier takes off his hat to him.

With a fortnight's experience much of the novelty of trench warfare had disappeared. One was absorbed mainly in ordinary campaigning pursuits, the desire for a change of diet, the hundred and one little every day devices that help to lessen discomfort and maintain physical fitness. There was the perennial problem of the little nuisances of life, the unbidden guests which come and abide with you—not as single spies, but in battalions. Had lice been sheep, many of us were squatters. The sight of the blue Aegean suggested fish and fishing, and our first experiment was with a tin of bully beef and a bomb. The tin was opened and thrown into the sea. Half an hour was given the fish to get interested, and the bomb followed the bait. The first catch was eleven fish up to 5 lbs in weight. On the following day we got over thirty, and the fish for breakfast as an alternative to fat bacon was just then one of the most desirable things in life. The only book I possessed—a translation of Dante's *Purgatorio*—seemed in one sense suited to the occasion and the scene. When nothing else was offered there was always the Turkish sniper and the wish to exchange compliments with him. One day, through over eagerness to get in touch with one of them, I laid myself open to crossfire from another quarter, and was given a lesson in prudence through the bridge of my rifle being shot away.

As bad luck had prevented me from seeing and sharing the beginnings of Gallipoli, the chances of war passed me out before the end of it. On the evening of November 5th—Guy Fawkes Day—our fireworks came in sudden and disastrous form. Sitting in company headquarters, which was roofed with iron and covered with about a foot of earth, I was giving some instructions to Sergeant Major James Purcell and Sergeant Fisher when a Turkish bomb found us. It was of a new pattern, made of shell casing filled with high explosive, and with a shaft some feet in length screwed to it. It burst immediately upon piercing the roof. Purcell, standing a little way off, was killed instantly. Fisher had, amongst other wounds, one of his hands badly mutilated. My injuries were chiefly on the back and crown of the head, eight serious shrapnel wounds in all, and a compound fracture of the skull. There was a wound in the right shoulder also, and the force of the blow seemed to have shot the right eye so far out of the socket that it had to be pushed back in again. Some fragments of iron lodged at the back of it even now causes complete loss of sight for a time.

It seemed the end of all things for the moment, but meant only the end of Gallipoli, and what touched me most on leaving it was the concern of the men with whom I had been more closely associated. In Egypt I had not been a tender taskmaster. There were times when I felt that my platoon hated me very cordially, that my death in or out of action would have caused them no grief. In two months of Gallipoli we had come to a better knowledge and understanding. I realised it then, realised it later when, although forbidden to boast about trophies of war, they managed to bring me out a few souvenirs of Gallipoli. Because of all that lay behind it, no gift that I ever received had a greater value.

A month of Malta and St John's Hospital followed upon that adventure and, with the help of a good constitution, I made a quick recovery. My flesh must, I think, have remarkable healing qualities, for the whole of my face, which was practically raw and disfigured when leaving Anzac, healed very rapidly and soon began to look normal again. Many fragments of Turkish metal which the x-rays revealed were not recovered by the surgeons, and still give occasional trouble.

I was able to see a little of this keep of the Mediterranean before leaving it, the tombs and memorials of the old knights of St John of Jerusalem, their armour and weapons in the armoury being of chief interest. Otherwise than in its fortress value and its old association with pilgrimages to the Holy Land—which seem, by the bye, to have been the carefully conducted Cook's cheap excursions of the period—Malta is not especially interesting. During convalescence I had a chance to visit Florence, but wished to get back to Egypt, wholly for the sake of meeting my brother Cecil and to arrange, if possible, for his transfer to my own corps.[4] It seemed to be highly desirable at the moment that my brother and I should be together, and headquarters were always willing to help out any such arrangement. Later I began to doubt the value of it, because in close companionship the anxieties about the other to devote himself to the single purpose, and there is always the chance that both may go out in the one calamity.

We had a sad illustration of that afterwards in the attack on Mouquet Farm. Captain Harold Smith let a company of the 22nd; his brother Captain Dick Smith had a company of the 21st. They went over the top together, and both were killed within a few yards of the parapet. A third brother, who had been badly wounded in the first attack, died in an English hospital a few days later, and the family tragedy was complete. All three were magnificent fellows—men in battle, gentlemen always.

Before reaching Cairo the wounds in my head had reopened, but a fortnight in hospital left me fairly fit for service, though with little hope of again seeing Gallipoli. Apart from the suggestive fact that reinforcements were no longer being sent to the peninsula, one had that definite sense of something impending. A dark cloud seemed to be gathering over the east, and those were not good days for anyone who happened for the moment to be outside the absorbing sphere of action. So the news that the great adventure had ended, that we had stolen away into the night, leaving our dead to the mercy of the Turk and the trenches, which he could never win in action, to his easy occupation, was not altogether a bolt from the blue. It was a melancholy ending to a magnificent effort. Into the strategic considerations which made evacuation desirable one may not enter without fuller knowledge of the circumstances, but the Anzacs of today have no self-accusing memories of it, no torturing sense of anything undone that might humanly have been accomplished. It brought them at least glory, well won in sacrifice. As one who shared only in a little of its story, it is possible to say so much without egotism, to say it for others as well as for Australians, because it is even now necessary to recall at times the splendid story of a certain 29th Division, though few on Gallipoli who had their eyes and ears open will need to be reminded of it. With the great story of Mons fresh in our ears, it seemed at the moment an unhappy fact that our shining things were being accomplished chiefly in retreats.

From the quiet confidences of camp and trench I knew how hard it was for the Anzacs to come away from Gallipoli, hardest of all to leave the little white crosses in the folds of the hills, where in their loneliness the lost lads lay waiting for the last daybreak.

> When across the mighty mountains
> And along the silent sea,
> The sublime celestial bugler
> Shall ring out the Reveille.

It had been a hard preparation for the greater phases to come, because there were no reliefs on Gallipoli, no billets behind the line—men were always in it and under it.

In camp again upon historic ground in the desert of Sinai, amongst the old trenches of Tel-el-Kebir, and hard by a cemetery filled with British dead. In the changeless east, shifting in many things—chiefly in sand—it was astonishing to find the old lines still so clearly marked. Just about that time I made the acquaintance of an Egyptian doctor, a very charming man, who on learning where we were camped chatted freely and interestingly upon incidents of the old campaign. That he was so familiar with every detail of that battle of thirty-three years ago was no longer a surprise when I found out that he was a nephew of Arabi Pasha, who fought us there.

Chapter 2

New battle grounds

With two companies of the rearguard of our expedition for France I left Egypt for the second time on the Khedival mail steamer *Osmanieh*, afterwards sunk by submarines. There was a second call at Malta, for a damaged screw sent us in for repairs, and we spent three days in port. In this delay, fate served us a good turn, for a boat, in company of which we should have been, was torpedoed. Without further incident we reached the great French naval fortress of Toulon—one of the most interesting places I have ever seen—early in March 1916, and afterwards steamed to Marseilles, where the Australians disembarked, and where we saw our first of the Bosche in some 8000 prisoners who were working about the docks. It was yet too early to see southern

France in its spring vesture, but after Egypt and Gallipoli any land in which green things flourished seemed beautiful. Very soothing it was to eyes so long accustomed to the grey pinnacles of the peninsula and the red of shifting desert sands, so the new adventure seemed to open with fairer promise.

The valley of the Rhône, cultivated to its last root with formal squares of hard-pruned orchards, lined in poplars and with vines clinging to every accessible niche of its rockiest hills, is charming at all seasons. We had been lifted from the world's nursery into the middle distance of medieval times amongst places such as Dijon and Tarascon, built up through centuries upon their own refuse, and with the medieval smell, which is decay accumulated and grown old, still lingering about them. Transfer from the crescent to the cross was pleasantly obvious in the little shrines which crown so many of the hill crests. The olive country was our only disappointment, for to the olive is given only the poorer soils of southern France and the grey-green of the groves by contrast of the verdancy of Rhône water meadows, still held some suggestion of that oriental sterility which we were but too willing to forget.

Travelling chiefly by day we had a fair glimpse of the pleasant fields of France, some acquaintance with the character of its historic towns like Lyons, the great silk centre, before we began to tread upon the heels of retreating winter again away north at Rouen by the Seine, after a hundred hours' journey through a land that has been washed and combed into cultivated beauty by many generations. Little wonder that the Frenchman is an ardent patriot, for his is a land that would have stirred even our home sluggards to action and sacrifice. Seeing it with new and eager eyes, we could realise all the meaning of that epitaph roughly scratched above the grave of a dead French soldier on the Somme:

My body to the earth,
My soul to God,
My heart to France.

It needed no troop trains to tell us that France was at war, for on that journey, which will live so long in memory, one saw few able-bodied men out of uniform. The day's work in France was being done chiefly by men bent with age, by women who, seen in the fields through the haze of early morning, recalled Millet's picture, *The Angelus* and by children. At some of the railway junctions we noticed even women engine stokers and cleaners— *Vivre la France!* With twenty-four hours in Rouen one had a chance to see some of the sights of the town, amongst them the beautiful Cathedral of Notre Dame—one of the few great northern churches which have been spared from the ruin of malignant German hate. We entrained next day for Berguette; a seven mile march at the end brought us to our billets at Wittes, and thence a few days later to the trenches of Fleurbaix, just south of Armentières, and within three hundred yards of the enemy, with whom every Australian was more anxious for a direct deal than he had ever been with Germany's hoodwinked tool, the Turk.

What a contrast to Gallipoli and the rainless Sinai desert were these waterlogged manways of the Western Front, with the tail end of a hard winter and occasional snow storms still biting into them. For eighteen months the tide of war had ebbed and flowed with little material gain either side. The proximity of the Hun had but hardened our hate of him, for that particular sector seemed to reek of his atrocities. We had fought the Turk as a formally declared enemy, without any particular animosity towards him; here it was altogether different. One must be blind to all the misery of martyred France, deaf to all authenticated tales of Hunnish depravity, here he could sit down with any degree of patience to wait for that which might happen.

It was early in April that we took over Fleurbaix from the 15th and 16th Royal Scots, and amongst other warnings given to us was, 'Look out for their patrols. They bombed us last night, and bombed us the night before. They're always bombing us in.' Fritz was presuming a bit considered that he had established a prowling right over the battle belt, but in less than a week he had given up possession.

The lure of night scouting, the silent, tense sensation of feeling one's way through the dark, groping for the unseen and unknown, began to get a grip of me again. It was sharpened up by resentment of the liberties which the Hun patrols were taking. Experimental patrols on three successive nights on no man's land served to strengthen a natural love for that particular work. If you meet an enemy the chances are that you meet him single-handed, matching the acuteness of your senses, your night craft against his. It is generally a fair deal, a fair duel, and he who is worst equipped for it takes the consequences. My first patrol was a prudent half-way to the German wires, and feeling about in the night for an hour and a quarter—rather than an experimental scour that one with any definite aim, for one needs to be quite sure of his nerves and the strain is constant. On the second occasion I left the patrol half-way and worked up close to the Bosche entanglements, repeating it on the following night.

Apart from personal liking for the job there was some purpose behind it. I was in charge of a party of three officers and seventy of other ranks (composed mainly of specialists such as grenadiers, machine-gunners and snipers) sent in ahead of the battalion to learn the line, and the best way to learn was by personal investigation. When news of my night promenades reached the ears of the commanding officer, a warning lecture followed. Officers could not be spared for that work, though before very long the need for it was fully realised.

Amongst our near neighbours were the Canadians, and news of the very effective scouting done by some of their expert backwoodsmen reached the ears of our divisional staff, who were so much impressed that they set about making special patrol arrangements. A lecture by a Canadian Captain, who had charge of the scouts of his own battalion, was being arranged, and attended by representative officers of each battalion in the division, as well as by headquarters staff. The Canadian was an expert in the job. With an enthusiasm that was infectious he urged the absolute necessity of scouting being properly organised as a battalion matter, instead of being casually undertaken just as the need or the impulse came. His arguments were, indeed, so convincing that the staff decided immediately to set about organising special patrols on the same lines as the Canadians. It was my good fortune to be given the job.

We realised that the work was both delicate and dangerous, and there was a call for volunteers. Of high courage there was no lack. The other requirement was keen intelligence, coupled with persistency. When complete, it was a command of which any officer might be proud; impressive less for its strength than for its qualities, a close companionship based upon mutual understanding. It was clearly understood that, if any man betrayed the confidence of his comrades, he should be shot, that if I failed them there should be no compunction in carrying out a sentence mutually self-imposed. A majority of the scouts were bush men.

Our first undertaking was to get absolute control of no man's land, representing at that point a breadth of about 350 yards between the rival fighting lines, to bar it to the Hun patrols, and, if possible, locate all their listening posts and machine-gun stations. On the very day that the scouts were organised the Brigadier had a job ready for us. The 24th Battalion reported that an unused trench, lying about a hundred yards in front of the enemy line, was believed to be occupied by them at night. We were to reconnoitre, bomb the Bosche out if they happened to be in possession, and fix up some sham protection to indicate that we intend to hold it. The hope was that on the following evening an enemy party would investigate, and with a machine gun trained on the position might spring a trap on them. We found the trench almost full of water, and with a canvas screen and sand bags fixed up, made it a fair imitation of a semi-circular redoubt. 'Will you walk into my parlour?' said the spider to the fly, but the fly, more suspicious than curious, declined the invitation.[5]

On the following night we crept towards the German wires, but within eighty yards of them an observer whispered that an enemy patrol of about twelve men had passed behind us towards our own lines. Retiring to our wires we sent in for the additional men and chased the Germans back to their trenches.

Night patrols on both sides are forbidden to bomb except in the last emergency, and the reason for it will be obvious. Their work is mainly investigation, and as it is impossible in the darkness to discriminate between friends and foe, supporting fire from either trench is impossible. So it was no uncommon thing to find two rival patrols, investigating each other curiously and silently through the dark with only a few paces intervening. Ours was, however, a bombing party, and having cleared the ground and dug shelter-holes just deep enough for fire cover, I took a Sergeant and two men, creeping right under their wires, we had the fatigue party absolutely at our mercy. With bomb pins drawn and the lever held down by the finger only, we could hear the low murmur of their conversation, apparently a party of about eight. They were so sure of themselves that some whistled softly at their work. On the signal four Mills bombs dropped on them, so beautifully placed that the burst suggested the position of stars in the Southern Cross. The whistling turned to an agonised scream.

That is a characteristic of the Hun. When surprised or hurt he screams. Our men take it sometimes silently, or with an exclamation, but frequently with an oath. Once you have heard a German scream he has lost caste in men company. On the moment the bombs were tossed we dashed for our funk holes, and then what a commotion! The German flares lit up no man's land, and their machine guns chattered across it but 'Brer rabbit he jes' lay low and dun say nuffin.' Safe from the storm that swished just overhead, we laughed in sheer enjoyment.

One immediate result of our night work was that the German patrols, originally composed of six men, were strengthened to twelve—they were 'getting the wind up.' There were few shell holes in that sector of no man's land. It was in the main a beautiful grassy stretch, and crawling through it at night one's face brushed against the first red poppies of Spring. In addition to passing our compliments—per favour of Mr Mills—to the Huns, we had been able to locate and take bearings upon the battle positions of two of their machine guns, though headquarters were dubious about it until they had confirmed our report by aerial observation. Then the emplacements were smothered in a burst of shell fire. For that interesting night's work our reward was the following note in the brigade orders:

Brigadier General Gellibrand has pleasure in placing on the record the excellent work carried out by the following patrol:—Lieut. W. A. Cull, Sergeant H. Payne, Privates O. Johnson and A. Cumstie.

Alexander Cumstie, who had fine qualities as a scout, was killed on the following night. I had great pleasure in recommending Herbert Payne, a solid, ever-reliable soldier, both for a decoration and promotion but the honours came too late. At Pozières soon afterwards he was sent to take a German strong post on the Bapaume Road. Twice he led his men against it, only to be beaten back with loss. Before leaving the trench for a third attack, he quietly shook hands with his friends and gave concise directions as to the disposal of his effects. His presentiment was justified, for he had only cleared the parapet when a bullet passed through his head, killing him instantly. Oscar Johnson was a strange contradiction, even in a force where character was often unusual. In Egypt and

Gallipoli he was always in trouble, for when he had looked a little while upon the wine that is red he could make more noise than a battalion. In France he was a particularly reliable man, and I picked him as a scout. And a fine scout he was, as game as they made. But leave was Johnson's folly. He would roar up the whole camp on his return, and with peremptory orders from the commanding office that it should be stopped, I told Johnson that he was going back to his company. Without a word he saluted, walked away, and the next I heard was that Johnson had forfeited and was laying for me with a rifle. For that indiscretion he was tried by court-martial, and heavily sentenced. A few days later he asked me to see him—not to intercede for him, he was careful to explain, as he had been a fool and deserved what he got. He wished to apologise, and on my application that sentence should be suspended, Johnson returned to the scouts. He came back, and proved himself a splendid man. He was soon wearing stripes and the ribbon of the Military Medal.[6]

A Gallipoli incident was recalled soon afterwards in a narrow shave from a Bosche shell, the wind of which dashed my hat off in the mud while I was worrying my way out of a trench with a wounded man.

As a general consequence of our night work the brigade intelligence officer was good enough to say that ours was the only battalion which knew its battle front thoroughly or had gained information of definite value to the brigade.

Chapter 3

War after dark

The detail of military work, though important, is not of itself interesting. While war is never without romance—as well as tragedy to which one never grows quite accustomed—the essence of that romance was still, with me, the night work. A patrol requires much detail to make it even in a small degree perfect, and for a while much of my time—apart from regimental duty—was given to perfecting my scouts in their essential detail. They had to be taught the value of simple speech, whether expressed by tongue or pen—what Kipling calls the 'straight flung words and few'— which heard or read can have but one meaning. Clearness is doubly essential when the message has often to be expressed in cipher. There were a score of other things to study and to teach before, with the best will in the world, scouting could become useful and explicit.

In the beginning I had deliberately taken risks which were sometimes perhaps unnecessary, but behind it was the definite object of convincing my men that, in whatever sense I failed them, it would not be through funk. In this night work, where the leader was wholly his own trumpeter, I was at any rate free from the suspicion of being a decoration hunter, which is the surest way of winning the contempt of your command. With a clear footing established comes caution and a sense of responsibility in the duty one owes to those who trust him. Thus far only one of my scouts had been 'crimed,' and crime is a very elastic work in military usage, yet so fine was their *esprit de corps* that the others sent him to Coventry immediately, and he had to be transferred back to his company.

We moved next to Armentières, where we relieved the 7th Brigade, and in between classes of instruction I was able to continue reconnaissance of our own particular sector, sitting night after night in the German wires until every tussock and hollow of that land, which was no man's in daylight and any man's after dark, became familiar. Equally familiar were the silences, the soft voices of the night—though often a bird, startled from the shelter of a tussock, seemed to our strained ears to make a perfect crash of sound. With such experience our self-reliance ever increased, and the men thought it good sport. There was no monotony. With air photographs as a basis we, in a few nights, became familiar with every ditch and drain, so completed a large sketch map showing every detail of the ground. We learned that the Bosche was accustomed to post two patrols at eleven each night, one in their front wires, the other just across a little creek. On more than one occasion we were lying right alongside that creek party without our presence being discovered.

Then came the raid for which all the scouting was a preparation, carried out by a company of selected men from each of the 22nd, 23rd and 24th Battalions, with the 21st in support to protect our flanks, lest the enemy should work around behind. I had command of the scouts, who were out early. One of our finds was a party of about thirty Germans hard at work cutting the long grass upon their front with scythes, so as to give them a clear field of fire. We were quite close to the mowers, who were a tempting target for bombs, but to have wiped them out, as we might easily have done, meant spoiling the raid. The creek, though narrow, was fairly deep, and duck boards were brought down to the bank and screwed together to bridge it, yet not a sound of the preparation reached the Hun patrol on the opposite bank. Our chief anxiety, as the hour for the raid approached, was that the mowers might hear our men approaching before they could reach their position, just near enough to the Hun wire to be clear of the back blast from the barrage which, with the 60 lb bombs used on the wire, means about sixty yards. Fortunately at the last moment they worked in towards their own wires.

The raid was timed to coincide with the relief of the enemy standing patrols, so that we could catch them en masse, and with our 60-pounders beat down their wire entanglements, exceptionally strong at that point, as we had reason to know.

In a sudden rendering and tearing of the silence of the night our trench mortars blazed out upon their entanglements, as we confidently hoped, and shells from guns of many calibres fell upon them. Four minutes after zero, the scouts, according to arrangement, crept forward as close as possible to their entanglements, which, seen faintly through the dark, seemed to me, ominously erect. As the barrage was lifted beyond we rushed upon the wires, only to find that through some extraordinary error in the range, not a wire had been cut in that particular area. Here was sudden and unexpected calamity, for their flares were already illuminating the darkness; in a little while every one of our raiders would be as clearly exposed to their machine guns as if in broad daylight.

Some of the scouts were at work with wire-cutters, though the chance of cutting through eighty yards of wire was about as forlorn a hope as men ever faced. In that emergency all the time and patience devoted to night scouting was in a moment justified. I remembered two saps which curved outward in crescent form through their wires, and took the one chance that offered—the possibility of getting into the Hun trenches by their own communications. Instead of cutting straight ahead, we started pulling up the wires down their length to reach the communication trench. It may be the excitement of such a moment, but, tearing up the wire with bare hands, we seemed to feel the barbs less than if gingerly threading our way through it at leisure. I had the luck to lob a bomb fairly under the first Hun we encountered, so close that he was shattered to death before he knew what hurt him.

That sap was the ready way to victory. We bombed the enemy down it to his main trench, though several of our fellows were hit just as we entered their front line. Then came a short and fierce struggle, but once we were fairly amongst them the Huns soon threw in the sponge. In such a mêlée Bavarians always made a better show than any other German regiments—not excepting the puffed up Prussians. Our men, with hands and faces blackened, and mud on their bayonets so that no chance flare should show them up on their way across, were certainly a terrifying sight, their charge carried through with the impetuosity that ever marks an Australian rush. Most of the enemy got away in a hurry to their support trenches. Amongst those who were not quick enough to escape, hands went up on all sides, and the craven cry of *'Kamerad!'* signified surrender.

The German is ever treacherous, and that night they paid the very limit the price of treachery. Three of them came from a dugout, holding up their hands, and as Sergeant Gordon Graham approached to take them prisoner, two of them suddenly dropped their arms, pulled out revolvers, and opened fire at the Sergeant at almost point blank range. One bullet passed through his ear, another through his left arm, a third went through his lungs and lodged within an inch of his heart. The Sergeant, as game a man as ever wore a uniform, quiet in speech as in manner, swore volubly for the first time in my hearing and brought down all three of the brutes with successive shots from his revolver as he collapsed. In that one act of treachery every German in the trench—in all about sixty men with two officers—pronounced his own death sentence. Not a man was spared. Fuming with just rage, every feeling of mercy in our fellows hardened in an instant to savage retribution. With bullet and club they sternly squared the account. Raiding parties carried at that time a heavy club—an iron cog-wheel attached to an entrenching tool handle—a silent, somewhat horrible weapon, not fit for a Briton to use in war, and rejected soon afterwards.

I had chased a German down the trench until, in a paroxysm of fear that could only invoke pity, he threw up his hands, trembling the while in terror. We had learned just sufficient German to assure a prisoner that if he surrendered no harm would come to him. To give him confidence I walked up and patted him on the shoulder, whereupon in fawning fear he stroked my face and wrung my hand, all the while chattering some inexplicable assurance. Docile as a child and still in deadly fear, he was handed over to one of my men to take back while I worked further down the trench. In the meantime the Graham incident had occurred, 'No prisoners' was the word, and the poor wretch died with the rest—our one satisfaction being that they were a Prussian regiment.[7]

All at once a wave of battle nausea, in the smell of blood, of death, of explosives and upturned earth, and the stale, foul odour of the trenches, surged over me, and in sheer dismay I thought, 'Good God! What is this poor old earth coming to?' However sadly you may have cause to reflect after battle, there's not much time for introspection on the very edge of it.

There was great temptation to push a success to completion, and in the excitement of action, with battle lust burning redly, men are not easily called off. Every detail of a raid, including the retirement, is timed with the nicest accuracy; there must be no independent action and, especially with success, no departure from the programme. Unwillingly they were withdrawn to find the angry enemy at midnight sweeping no man's land with unavailing fire. They had rushed back when the barrage lifted, were making most of the occasion in shouting 'Hands up!' to imaginary enemies who were then in their old rendezvous by the creek side, snug and safe. When they came in later a good many wore German helmets.[8]

Nothing connected with the events of the night gave me greater satisfaction than the fact that Sergeant Graham survived his wounds. Bad as they were, I had to ask him to get back to the lines, and then command him to do it—finally to have him carried back. It was a long carry for the Sergeant too, out of the trenches and battle front, and right back to the farm home in Australia which is dignified in the possession of a man whom all his intimates value as a stalwart fighter in war, their personal kinks and crudities all forgotten in love of the brave, strong hearts beating underneath. In war one doesn't wear his heart upon his sleeve, but we all, I think, understood 'To each a mate who knows his naked soul.' You find him in all shapes and ranks—sometimes a brigadier, sometimes a batman.[9]

It was as batman and a scout that I got to know Private Jones, who, as a shearer in Australia, had roughed it over a great part of the continent. With him life was largely a bivouac. He had learned to make the best of every condition, however cheerless. One perishing cold night, when we held the line in an emergency without kit, I was stamping and jumping about trying to keep the circulation active, when Jones came out of his wombat-hole.

'Can't you sleep, Captain?' he asked.

'How can one sleep in this cold without blankets?' I replied.

'No blankets?' he said in wonderment. 'What sort of batman have you got? I'll soon get you a pair of blankets.'

'You won't do anything of the kind—do you think I'm going to take yours?'

'It's all right, I can spare them. I've got five pairs.'

'Where did you get them?'

'Better not ask Sir.'

Later I did ask, but with a slightly different inflection, and Jones explained that he had carried down some imaginary wounded to the dressing station and borrowed blankets from the store to make them comfortable.

As fine a skirmisher as he was a scout, Jones became my batman on the earliest possible opportunity and in foraying or foraging was a pearl. A primus stove and cooking utensils came as if by jugglery. When there should have been only an iron ration, Jones produced eggs and bacon. As a purveyor he was one long, delightful surprise. He had the high Australian estimate of mateship. For the sake of it was prepared to beg, borrow or steal. After a night stunt there were always dry clothes waiting—very often a grilled beefsteak, which on one occasion I found he had gone four miles to obtain. He had a solid service record, and won the Military Medal. Only a few nights before I was taken prisoner I managed to get Jones a comfortable job with the quartermaster, and it was a satisfaction afterwards to know that he was out of the battle line.[10]

Chapter 4

On the Somme

Following another interlude of regular duty in which we took our part in the attack on Pozières Ridge on July 30, I soon afterwards, with the rank of Captain, was transferred to the 22nd Battalion, which had lost so many of its regimental officers, and was given command of a company. The first day of importance had more risks than glory, the control of a carrying party taking ammunition from the reserves to the forward dumps. Day and night we passed through the German barrage, learned to appreciate the strength of their gunnery and the accuracy of their range. It was a terrible task accompanied with heavy casualties. Our artillery had fortunately increased. At Fleurbaix we had been able to hand back only one shell to every eight given us by the enemy;

at Pozières we were giving them two shells for one. Our air scouting, too, had improved marvellously in daring and effect. The flyers often waved their arms to us in greeting as they dipped low to gun the Bosche in their trenches. Thick as wasps they were and as successful in spotting German gun emplacements as our counter battery fire was cleaning them out. German prisoners seemed more than ever pleased to be out of it. One day, as a party of them were taken past our lines, an officer waved his arm and shouted, 'Cheerio, old birds! I'm off to Donington Hall to play tennis until the end of the war. You fellows carry on as usual.'[11]

Another batch of German prisoners brought in from Sausage Valley was not so cheerily indifferent; and little wonder, for they had an unholy fright. As they neared our kitchens out poured a detachment of cooks, each armed with a huge carving knife, and made a dash for their victims. The handsomest and most self-attentive man in the British Army looks something of a ruffian disfigured by a few days' stubble upon his face and all the stain of the trenches, but a military cook, in all his panoply of grease and rags, is the very incarnation of ruffianism. The prisoners were limp with fright. Even I for a moment thought the cooks had suddenly gone mad and contemplated murder, but it was only a dash for souvenirs, and for every button that they slashed away they considerately handed the former owner of it a cigarette. Big, well-nourished men were these German prisoners, with never a sign of the spectacled savant or undeveloped boy by which the illustrated papers served up to us as the sign of German deterioration. If the Hun civilian was being starved, the soldier was well fed. Captured trenches gave sufficient proof of that. His biscuits were not as nourishing as ours, and easier to eat, he had still tinned meats in abundance, stacks of sausages which, if greasy, seemed palatable, and they habitually used bottled soda water for drink in the trenches.

Behind the lines one had a chance of again noting the patient heroism with which the French peasant went on his way in the very teeth of war, permitting nothing to disturb for a moment his ingrained thrift. Quiet, simple folk, trading profitably with our men, mainly through the convenient medium of pantomime, one had to get behind their skin of stolid indifference to realise a soul aflame with patriotism.

Just thereabout I had a subordinate share in a resolute bit of work standing the credit of Captain Maberly Smith of the 23rd Battalion. In an attack the battalion won its ground, but the flanking corps failed, leaving our right flank in the air and dangerously exposed, so he was told to retire. To give up ground because of the failure of others was not to the Captain's taste. 'Oh, be damned!' he said. 'The battalion doesn't retire.' Rudely ignoring the order, which may have been only a suggestion, he dug round on that side for flank protection and hung on grimly for several days until the debatable ground on our right was won and line restored.[12]

We located and fully accounted for a strong post which the enemy had formed across the Bapaume Road. Having carefully reconnoitred the position, we placed machine guns in position and, with the range carefully ascertained, opened up on them in daylight with the Stokes gun; a deadly bit of ordnance with fire so rapid that eight 12-pounder shells are in the air together. It was too hot for Carl, and as he rushed out the machine guns cut him down. Apparently we accounted for the lot, about sixty Huns being found dead, and searching them we got on the body of an officer the report which he was about to send in—'To the House of the Brigadier, I have this night taken in front of the Australians a strong post across the Bapaume Road.' On another of their dead were photographs and papers taken from one of our own sentries who had mysteriously disappeared. In this case Nemesis was prompt.

In this story it should be understood that there is no pretence of chronological order, just an impression of observations and incidents written as they are recalled, with a memory somewhat blurred since by the effect of a German bomb and after effects of German hate, but amongst them some vignettes of battle that can never become obscure, since with so much of the glory of battle is mixed up its ghastliness.

On the Somme we were twice 'over the bags' in something more imposing than trench fighting, with casualties for the division heavier, it was believed, than any regiment had endured since Mons. We were very tired of trench warfare then, though fighting in the open would have deprived us of an underground companionship of rats, mice and other inevitable creatures, to whom we act chiefly as hosts. Like a friendly dog the rat trots about your dugout by night, often treading trustfully upon your face. In the open above they are in swarms, sharing by daylight our watchfulness, though parapet and parados be honeycombed with their funk-holes. Almost a domestic animal was the French rat, with nothing of the ill-bred haste of our city dweller in drains and docks. They were wise rats in a way, with no love for shell-torn country.

Apart from the crowded hours of actual battle, nothing on the Somme was more impressive than the first sight of our guns in the open—an immense concentration, each type in line, first the 60 lb mortars, then field guns, and so on, in successive lines, receding further to the rear as range and power increased, a companionship of calibres in 6, 8, 9 and even 12-inch cannon.

On one occasion, with an English company attacking on our flank, it was our duty to keep the Huns' heads down for them—in military language, to cover their attack with machine gun fire. The attack was knocked back and I was never more amazed in my life than when the officer commanding came to us with the astounding request:

'Will you fellows take that trench for us?'

'Oh, go to the devil!' I retorted. 'We have had a fair thing already.'

'But your fellows like attacking,' he protested. 'You could do it easily enough.'

He persisted, even to the pretence that it was ordered, but without a written command we declined to oblige, though, when his company again attacked, quite a number of our Hotspurs hopped over with them.

If there were not two sides to that picture be sure that one side would never have been revealed. It seems to be a convention of war that even those familiar with it should never speak too freely of its emotional side, speak only of it in terms of broad and blazing glory, such as those favoured by very peaceful men obsessed of a duty in war orations, the flamboyant stuff used by a sick Kaiser to hearten up a beaten army.

There are phases of war, when the God of Battles is 'sifting out the hearts of men before His judgement seat' that are stranger than fiction, more impressive than slaughter. Judging from too hasty impulses, such an incident as that just related, one might fear at times that England was 'losing its punch' did he not notice that England never lowered its guard. It seemed incredible that an English officer should expect or ask Australians to undertake his job, but that very same regiment showed a silent, uncomplaining endurance in sitting under an eruption of German shell, with all its unimaginable horrors, that no soldiers whom I have ever seen in action could surpass. Let it be sufficient for our fame that, in the very crisis of the great enemy advance, three of our divisions before Amiens rolled back the German waves, started an ebb in the tide of war which never after changed to flood. Still we recognise that in some phases of war we have our limitations, and these happen to be just the particular phases in which Englishmen have no peers. I have seen our men sitting under a barrage, some of them reading their Bibles in anticipation of immediate death, others quite nerve-broken and tearful, some very near the verge of madness. It is all a question of temperament—the highly strung, impulsive Australian, with whom initiative has become a life habit, doing his best in one way, the less imaginative, enduring Briton doing it in another. It seems a little strange that springing from one stock two nations should in a few generations have so diverged.

The Briton, with long record of glorious achievement, needs but resolve to maintain and live up to those deeds which have made the name such a proud one, while we, as the cubs from a new land, with a consequent poverty of local traditions, were determined in our debut on the stage, where history is made and national characteristics are established, to prove worthy the great stock whence we sprang and, if possible, in our enthusiasm to excel.

Of course other and greater reasons contribute a more far-reaching cause of the difference. Ours was a wholly volunteer force and, consequently, the men were carefully chosen—the flower of our country—whereas conscription carried into the ranks of Great Britain's armies a percentage of men who, though keen and devoted to their country, would not have been considered mentally or physically fit, according to our standard of enlistment. It also forced into the ranks the usual quota of those who had no inclination to risk their lives.

The psychology of war is made up of many moving human factors. Distorted by intense strain, its manifestations take forms generally unexpected, often almost humiliating. The best antidote to fear is that pride of race which forbids us to fail, and it shines better in fierce activities than in slow, solid endurance.

It had long been my desire to get my brother Cecil into my own company, but an incident of a night on the Somme changed that view. Relieved about two o'clock in the morning, and bivouacking anywhere, I had thrown myself down to sleep, when about five in the morning the waterproof sheet was gently pushed back from my face and I felt a hand upon my forehead. It was my brother, whom I believed to be still in hospital with an injured ankle. With brothers in the same corps and going over the top together, the thoughts and fears of each are too much with the other. They get dopey, can neither dodge danger nor do their duty so efficiently as when alone.

At Ypres we held Sanctuary Wood, the burial ground of so many great Canadians who stood up to the mystery and horror of the first chlorine gas attack. I had just sufficient gas on one occasion to realise something of their fate. It was three o'clock in the morning when the gas came over, and on a long frontage men were so scattered that it was only tear shells, but soon one was screaming with pain. In trying to get one man up I had to take off my helmet for an instant. Almost instantly there was a smothering, burning feeling, but a fortunate sudden sickness saved me from its worst consequences. The trenches themselves were a continuous horror—mud up to the knees, sometimes to the thighs, wounded men at times sinking into its deadly smother as though they were held in quicksands. I had a sector of six hundred yards of sheer sorrow on the Somme; a garrison of eighty men to risk body and soul in the keeping of it, for our orders were to hold it to the last man. A trench was considered passable or possible when it held no more than 3 feet 6 inches of water, and of our six hundred yards two hundred were considered 'possible'. It was one night in this sink of desolation that I received a letter from my mother which recalled Bairnfather's happy idea about 'that blinkin' moon' for in the dim light I read, 'How I would love to be with you now.' It's just as well that mothers don't always know.

No really big game—and war is the supreme game—is without its omens, coincidences and superstitions. As November 5th approached, comrades warned me more than once to take care. 'If you're to go out, that's your night,' they said. It was on November 5th that I was wounded at Gallipoli. It was all ridiculous, of course, but thoughts for which there is no accounting, which would never stand the searchlight of reason in everyday life, come to you in war—and stay. So on November 5th I did not enter the dug-out all day. After dark I got out of the trench too, stayed out in the open while it snowed, and after midnight went back to sleep with some little feeling of shame, perhaps, but a certain satisfaction in having for the moment given Fate the slip. Many such presentiments have been realised in battle, because many men have them. I returned from leave in England with a full conviction that the next would be my last fight, and made every preparation for 'the journey West.' There was hard fighting, and I came through unscathed. On the other hand, I went into what proved to be my last fight with a firm conviction that, whoever might fall, I should not. Such are the presentiments which many soldiers know that sometimes happily go astray.

There was a disposition at that time to credit the Hun with exceptional skill and daring in espionage to magnify his cunning and minimise our own. When a certain unit took Bayonet Trench and lost it forty-eight hours later, we were given beforehand the exact time when the enemy would come over, and the intelligence was confirmed in the event.[13] Similarly on taking over from a British regiment at Le Boeuf, we had smiled at the CO's warning: 'You'll take over at midnight. In the early morning the Huns will endeavour to raid the trench held by the company on your left. Make your dispositions to meet it.'

It seemed a climax in absurdity. Did the Hun leave it to us to time his raids and elaborately prepare his programme? Later the disbelieving smile changed to wonder, because the enemy kept his appointment to the minute, and as good hosts we had a warm greeting waiting for him. One night we had a message in code giving us the exact hour at which the enemy would bring reliefs to his front line trenches, and guns were laid on to catch him in the confusion of change. Again it came off, as we found out from a badly rattled Bosche, one of the victims, who walked into our line by mistake in the early morning.

It was at Gueudecourt that we had our first experience of a northern winter. Snow storms were frequent, the cold, in spite of our sheepskin coats, often so keen as to be a pain, and one began to realise for the first time some of the meaning and miseries of polar exploration. Because we knew so much less than the Briton what frost-bite meant, trench feet became so common, casualties so high, that it was necessary to take drastic measures. It was the duty of a company commander to inspect his men's feet every day, to see that they changed into dry socks when opportunity offered, soaked their feet in whale oil, and had at least one hot meal a day. Here the Tommy Cookers were invaluable. With each of them was issued a tin of solid alcohol that looked like jelly, and a tin of Maconochie rations serves four men, with hot tea in a Dixie. There was a soup kitchen close to the line, in charge of the padre, where one could get hot soup any hour of the day or night. One result of strict supervision was that the Australians, originally censured for having so many men put out of action for trench feet and frostbite, gradually worked to the stage where they were congratulated instead upon fewer casualties in that way than any other army on the Western Front. That happy result was only brought about by the cooperation of all ranks.

In another direction this all-round cooperation worked very happily. I had hit upon the idea of arranging for entertainments in winter billets, believing that it would help keep the men out of the villages and out of trouble. There was little sympathy for the idea at first. We sent gun limbers five miles to cart in a piano, and rigged up a barn as a concert hall. Out of the success of this movement grew the determination to have a company Christmas dinner at Flesselles, to which two hundred and eighty men sat down, on the clear understanding that crime was suspended for the evening. The Don Dinner was one of our proudest accomplishments, and it did not end with the dinner. Out of the finer *esprit de corps* established grew a higher standard of conduct.

Chapter 5

Another night stunt

Short leave and a flying visit across the Channel was a pleasant break in winter warfare. December is not quite the best time of the year, though, to get one's first impressions of England. Surprise at the apparent familiarity of everything in the big city was the first feeling. Trafalgar Square, the Embankment, the Monument, the Abbey, even Whitechapel left one with the feeling that he had come back after many years to something familiar in a former existence. It was rather the sense of renewing old associations than of forming new ones. So other Australian soldiers who saw England in the flowing time of the year found, not only in its City lions, but in its quiet rustic lanes and hedgerows places where neither bird nor flower were strange, and felt that same suggestion of 'auld lang syne'. One would like to imagine it the Cradle Call of the Race, though poetry, painting and the prose of historian, naturalist and antiquarian, all unconsciously absorbed, are perhaps the real factors of familiarity. That, after all, is only another way of stating the facts, without disturbing the fancy.

Travelling to Scotland on the Great Northern Railway one day I had as companions two aged gentlemen, one of whom, an American master engineer with eight hundred men in his control, remarked that the railway luncheon baskets were not up to the standard.

'I expect, though,' he said, 'they're a sight better than what you have in the trenches.'

'Yes, decidedly better,' I replied. The second traveller seemed to shake off his indifference.

'You get much better food than that,' he asserted. I explained that I was not grumbling—rather otherwise—but tried to explain that we were not habitually set up to ham and chicken, asparagus, fresh rolls and butter, with wine to wash it down. He relapsed into indifference again, but a little later casually remarked that he was with Lord Davenport, as a Director of Food Supply to the British Army on the Western Front.

On my return to the Somme front after leave, my company was in reserve for a while before the Butte de Warlencourt, and there the old Gallipoli wounds broke out again and caused some trouble. After a few days in hospital I joined up again just in time for one of those night stunts, the mystery and adventure of which were ever a strong appeal. Personal interest in the undertaking was sharpened by the presentiment that the next fight was to be the end of the passage. So strong was the conviction that I went through my valise, cleared up all my papers, and wrote a card home to be posted in the event of my death.

We had been four days and nights in the trench and were about to be relieved by the 7th Brigade, when instructions came from headquarters to detail a strong reconnoitring party to move out in the darkness, get in touch with the enemy and find out his strength and dispositions. I sent out first a light patrol, which returned in about an hour and reported that all the indications showed that the Huns were holding the line in considerable strength, and that their front was heavily covered with wire. This was reported to Headquarters, who almost immediately ordered that a strong patrol should be sent out with instructions to penetrate the enemy line. No reasons were given for this extraordinary direction, beyond the remark that if only one man got back with the necessary information it was worth the sacrifice. All of them got back with the information that it was quite impossible to get through the barbed wire entanglements. The report was still unsatisfactory, and the next order was to send out three strong patrols, which meant practically the whole available strength of the company, and pierce the wires at three separate points. This time they carried machine guns. With only about eight men remaining in the trench at that point, I asked permission to lead the attack, but was ordered to stay at the telephone and report as soon as any information was received.

It was a long wait and a trying one, more wearing and worrying than action. For two hours I waited without a sound from the front to indicate either success or discovery. No message came; no man returned from out of the blackness, there was no break in the tension but the ever worrying insistence of Headquarters for information. It was a relief when the order finally came to take the whole of my company and attack at one o'clock.

It was then for the first time that I got some idea as to the reason for action. There was a belief that the enemy had retreated right along our sector, that the main German Army was thirty miles back, and that he was merely holding the trenches in front with a skeleton force which would retire on the first demonstration. I asked whether there was any mistake about the order, because no word had come from the front; they seemed to have disappeared utterly. The company with which I was to attack, as they must be aware, reduced to a strength of eight of all ranks, and to advance with such a handful and without artillery preparation, was to invite a fiasco. I was told to send down a runner as a guide, and the second in command would come up and see what could be done. In the black night the runner lost his way. Five men were sent into no man's land to try and get touch of the lost patrols, but still no word came back. Finally, in sheer desperation, I said: 'Come on, Sergeant Major. It's one o'clock and we must attack. Get the bombs.'

Feeling cautiously along the front we came upon our missing patrols, sheltering in an abandoned trench under the German wires.

'What are you doing there?' I asked.

'We can't get through the German wires, Sir,' was the reply.

After the worry of the last couple of hours I was not in a particularly amiable mood, and retorted: 'Do you think that, if you sit there looking at them, the wires will fall down or fly away?'

Scouts were sent out with instructions to try and find a passage, however small, though it permitted but one man to go through at a time. There was no success. A second patrol returned with reports just as discouraging, and finally I went forward with a man to investigate. There was just one point in our favour, the one thing which had saved us from discovery. Usually the German protective wires were not more than fifteen paces in advance of their trench. At Butte de Warlencourt, a little flat topped ridge formed the front German line, and the contour of the ground compelled the enemy, in order to get a better field of fire, to put his entanglements about fifty yards out from his fighting post.

His front line of wire was wholly on the 'knife rest' pattern, prepared in sections, so that, instead of boring in with auger pegs and crisscrossing the wires between them, the lengths of defensive wire already prepared may be carried forward separately and placed in position end to end. Beyond this, I found later, was a band of low apron wire about twelve feet in width. By burrowing away at the junction of the knife rest sections I discovered that it was possible to force them just far enough apart to make room for one man to crawl through. The patrols nearly a hundred strong were mustered at that point. Whispered instructions were passed along to plaster the bayonets with mud, so that in the event of flares going up the light gleaming upon the steel should not betray our position.

The plan was that I should crawl through the wires and, immediately on getting inside them, drop down. Each successive man who followed was to drop down on either side of me until the whole company was extended and ready for attack. The surprise was almost as complete as one could wish it, but through anxiety or over-eagerness, the last few men blundered into the apron wire, which twanged like banjo strings in the darkness. The German sentry knew the significance of that sound. He immediately challenged and fired, but before they could do much more I shouted the order to charge, and the company rose and dashed for their trench.

Quite obviously they had no warning this time of our visit, indeed we had little notice of it either. A few bombs were thrown; they waited until we were within thirty yards, and then ran like scared rabbits. With a few casualties to a unit on the left which met some opposition, we broke into the trench and bombed down the bays which, placed at intervals of about thirty yards, were especially roomy. With a few men I followed the enemy for about fifty yards beyond the trench. They stayed not upon the order of going, but went at once, making barely a show of fight. That is the way of the Hun. When assured of his strength, or his advantage in position, he will 'stick it' as well as the next. But when the unknown comes to him suddenly out of the darkness the superman softens, and all his iron turns to putty. A few of us chased him for fifty yards beyond his line with little hope of catching up, and the work of more immediate necessity was to consolidate and hold what we had won.

Here was an instance where what seemed to be an almost helpless adventure had, with a little luck and a lot of pertinacity, turned out almost a bloodless success. Feeling that I was being a bit unfairly blamed for circumstances beyond control, I was fuming with rage, determined to force a way through or over the wires at all cost, even though it had to be done by carrying over the duck boards from our own trench and throwing them across the enemy wire to bridge a passage. That was a last extremity and, with the flares up and the machine guns sweeping us at point blank range, would have meant heavy casualties.

In the brief trench turmoil I had lost my steel helmet, wound a woollen comforter round my head and armed with a German rifle which one of the enemy, in his eagerness to get quickly off the mark, had thrown away, I must at the moment have looked rather more like a Turk than a Briton. I was quite aware when, as I left half the company forward later to work around the village of Warlencourt, that my men were finding much amusement in the spectacle. I was probably the first Britisher amongst the ruins of Warlencourt, where the Germans as usual, had left 'the mark of the beast'.[14]

Chapter 6

Psychology of battle

War, as the greatest game in the world, has a psychology all its own, and in its tense phases, the great crises, its emotions are mainly primitive. Much has been written upon the heroics of battle, very little of its depths, of the strange and wholly unexpected things that happen when men are tried to the breaking point. Civilisation seems to slip away very easily under that searching fire-test, the original man is revealed apart from all that culture may have done for him, and the revelation is often disconcerting. One's impressions on this subject are necessarily personal, but I have discussed it with comrades and found, in their impressions and experiences, unanimity so remarkable that one is able to speak broadly of emotions as the rule of battle. If the reader unfamiliar with war is occasionally shocked, the conventions upon which he has been nourished are to blame. War has its heroic side in sacrifice, but in the main it is brutal. No one with experience of it may honestly pretend otherwise. Amongst its mixed emotions are some that are almost degrading

No better battle ground for the analysis of emotion can be chosen than the long, bitter struggles for the Ridge of Pozières, where about Gibraltar our white crosses now stand, arm to arm, in line and square, and where a fit memorial has been raised to Australian valour and sacrifice. It is a spot sacred to Australians, especially so to the soldiers who fought there. I am told that, in the last great German advance, the one resolve that fired our troops to iron resolution was: 'They must never get Pozières.' It was the crosses and the men and the memories lying beneath that appealed. 'Who, being dead, yet speaketh.' Its battle tests were supreme, presented the two great phases in effort, the rush against positions that bristled with death and difficulty, the long tenacity of hanging on under such a torrent and torment of shell fire as Australian fighters had never previously visualised or experienced.

In going up for our first innings at Pozières we were aware that the First Division had been in action and had lost heavily. For many days there had been foreknowledge of something very big just ahead. It was indicated in the many letters written home which I had to censor, and they showed where thoughts centred in that supreme hour of suspense. The keynote was ever the same, and I make no apology for breach of trust in revealing it. 'My dear mother, this is the eleventh hour.' To so many of those, whose thoughts flew far, there was no dawn to follow the midnight. My personal feeling at the moment was one of unshaken faith in the unit, doubt only as to myself. Self-introspection brought always the same question: 'Will I prove worthy of the Battalion?'

In front of us was the heavy Bosche barrage, varying in depth from 200 to 400 yards, bursts of white from the shell and, piercing up through the centre of it, the black earth spurts. To pass through it without annihilation seemed impossible. We saw a shattered British battalion come back, noted how its units had shrunk almost to nothing. In face of such evidence there could be little comfort and no indifference. Here again was the personal conviction that, although the enemy must lose heavily, I was certain to pass unscathed, and in conversation afterwards with other officers I found that they had exactly the same feeling. Men were very serious then, though many tried to bluff it through with forced jokes, and, with a big thing ahead, it takes a big bluff to cover it. Everyone who has had a fair share of trench fighting knows the great anomaly. Heavy and continuous shell fire, whatever the casualties, is demoralising, nerve shattering. The chattering of machine guns are by far the greater peril, yet men go up light-heartedly in face of one and wilt despondently under the lesser but more awesome danger.

At one point of the advance we passed a shell hole eruption from the piled earth of which a dead shrunken blackened arm was thrust out gruesomely, with the stiffened fingers extended. One laughing devil as we passed placed a tin of bully beef in the extended hand, with the remark, 'Get up you loafer—we're doing your work!' It was the big bluff, in normal circumstances would have been instantly resented as something too gross even for war. But under such a strain men both do and say things which would revolt them in ordinary life, and the man who can be coarsely light-hearted, either in assault or endurance, is at that moment a greater moral asset than the quiet thinkers of finer fibre. Never was that conviction so fully realised as in the tense period of waiting for a big German counter attack, where the word has passed that in no circumstances must there be retirement. On such an occasion I had passed down the line and put the position briefly, you will say perhaps brutally, but this was not a school for the cultivation of the graces and refinements. It was war, imperiously direct in its demands, and with success dominating every other consideration.

'We expect a big counter attack at any moment,' I said, 'and no man must go back, no one yield a yard of this trench. If we beat them back with the machine guns, no one must hop out of this trench to follow them up. We don't quite know each other yet. I don't know myself. If I want to leave this trench, kill me. One thing, however, I promise you. The command to retire can only be given in this sector by me, and I tell you, by all that I hold sacred, the word shall never be spoken. If you hear it, ignore it. It won't come from me.'

In the strain of waiting that trench was a medley of mixed emotions. Where thoughts flew backwards one saw quiet tears trickling down drawn, trench-stained faces. It is a bad time for the fighting man, a bad time for his mission. Through the mass of humanity that leaven of loving softness spreads far too easily. It is one of the reasons why 'Home, sweet home' and other tender melodies are banned as battle songs, why one should never take photographs into the front line, or look at them when he is there. Far better at such a time to get home and the home folk out of the mind, if one is to concentrate every thought, every energy upon the big absorbing job in hand. I say, with considerable experience, that in such a crisis the presence of men here and there who let themselves go without shame or reserve, curse the enemy loudly, continuously, brutally, are a greater asset, a finer stiffener to a smitten, sniffering line than thirty per cent of reinforcements. You find and hear them in unexpected places, and without social distinction. It may be a navvy or a bank clerk; the one at the moment is neither better nor worse than the other; there is, save in the continuance of authority, no distinction between the officer and the man. The cultivated graces have been shed away, the primitive man is uppermost. Civilisation has lost hold for the moment, savagery is almost supreme. It seems shocking that a man may be hurried to judgement with an oath scarce cold upon his lips. To those who may and will be shocked, who have nursed themselves afar with the fake little illusions of life, I can only suggest that the creator and controller of men knows the nature of his handiwork, its strength and its deficiencies, and, in the great eruption which has laid both bare, his judgement may be merciful.

And he who toss'd thee down into the Field
He knows about it all. He knows! He knows!

I hurry, for comforting contrast, to that other extreme, the magnificent brotherhood of battle. It warms and grows and glows into being very slowly and always under long continued strain, ever impending calamity. It is a brotherhood finer, I think, than anything else in the whole human world. The roughest become gentle under its influence, all selfishness disappears. You have an overpowering impulse to put your arm around your next man's neck, to say something decent, human and gentle. It is the love of suffering man for his fellows in suffering, the last and greatest phase of battle emotions surviving all the earlier, dangerous impulses of which I have spoken. It is the time when the officer who understands rises to the occasion and is idolized. At such a time would Brigadier General Gellibrand pass along the trench, and his quiet, 'Box on, boys! Stick it out!' was in similes which they understood as an inspiration. At such a time the true leader is at once a commander and a comforter, in very truth the trusted father of his boys.

Going in for the first big test, one naturally meets the troops coming out who have been through the trial. The first impression is that every man has been doped and drugged with rum. Men stagger about drunkenly; they seem to lose all sense of direction. If spoken to they answer curtly, confusedly, in monosyllables. They are really drugged with battle, but there is nothing either exalting or ludicrous in such intoxication: it is something seen in others rather than self-comprehended. You in your turn will, after many days in the front line, come out in exactly the same mentally muddled state, yet personally unconscious of it. The further exhausted troops are removed from the battle line, the more quickly they recover their mental poise. That state of drugged drunkenness lasts generally from twenty-four to forty-eight hours. Their only wish, then, is to be left alone.

> *All things are taken from us and become*
> *Portions and parcels of the dreadful past;*
> *Let us alone! What pleasure can we have*
> *To war with evil? Is there any peace*
> *In ever climbing up the heaving wave?*
> *All things have rest and ripen towards the grave,*
> *In silence ripen, fall, and cease*
> *Give us long rest or death, dark death or dreamful ease.*

Just here comes the irony of custom, a usage which at first sight seems to be nothing short of thoughtless barbarity. Next day these tired troops are marched to a parade ground to be put through the simpler elements of a drill with which they are absolutely familiar. Men are naturally intolerant and angry, and as they rarely pass the blame for any injustice beyond their immediate commander, he becomes for a time the best hated man in the battalion, in their estimation a merciless, exacting tyrant. Here again is considered method, the lessons learned in the long sequence of Great Britain's great and little wars, the applied wisdom of men who have made soldier mentality a life study. Both from a mental and military point of view, it is desirable that men should be doing something, be lifted out of themselves, and the ABC of the drill ground serves the purpose as well as anything else.

In war as in most other energies, the strength of the chain is the weakest link, and the breaking of the weak link is the constant apprehension of the commander, for with the mettle and the spirit broken, all sense of shame and decency disappears. False commands will be passed on and panic, that strange thing which spreads like a fire even amongst the bravest, may be on the verge of ignition. Such instances are very rare, while they continue very dangerous, for men are not mentally fit to consider the possibilities or probabilities of an order. As a rule the offenders are men of imagination who have broken under strain, are to be pitied than blamed, though in a war trench pity has, for the moment, no footing. As a company officer I have heard the command, which I had never given, passed along until in reaching men communications were broken, and the fault corrected. In such a state few men, and a few only, began to see things that have no existence, that are the fantasy of a bloodshot eye and tottering mind.

There were such instances as we say under the fiercest barrage I ever experienced in that unforgettable K Trench, looking up the slope to the blazing enemy crest of the Ridge of Pozières. It was the greatest concentration of artillery, and we sat under it. The noise of passing and bursting shells, of guns of all calibres, made one continuous appalling roar, until as a trench humorist said, 'One more shell as a keystone, and the whole lot will interlock and make an iron roof overhead.' Shells, which burst close at hand, were seen, a pillar of flame by night, a black earth tower by day, but not heard as something apart from the tumult of sound. One very general hallucination of the moment was that all these guns were German. I had to point out again and again that we were giving them two shells for one, to remind them of the great array of guns we had seen as we passed through the shelter of Sausage Valley, to point out the spires that darted up by hundreds and disappeared again in the grey haze shrouding the Hun positions.

'Send up the S.O.S. flare!' was a false command more than once given. One man could see waves of German stormers advancing to the assault, where not a human being was visible. He had no desire to run, even when forward over the parapet to fire on them. The S.O.S. flares, only to be used in a last emergency with the enemy visible in such strength that we had no mortal hope of holding them, were fortunately in my possession. The flare would have brought down a barrage of bursting iron between us and the enemy, but there must be no call for it without the most urgent reason: to seek it without sufficient cause would have been to disgrace the battalion.

As suddenly as if by mutual consent of both sides the great bombardment, with its torrent of iron, its tumult of noise, died away, and for a while the silence was even more nerve-racking than the sound. Everyone had the sense of something great and mysterious impending; some new deviltry just about to burst.

Reinforcements, which reach the front line for their baptism of fire just when a great battle is in progress, are facing perhaps the greatest trial to which a human being may be subjected. It seems to be the rule of the ranks to offer them cold comfort and a speedy release from all earthly concerns. I remember as vividly as anything our own experiences as novices at Gallipoli. Our first real battle thrill came as sudden as a revelation at Heliopolis in Egypt when the band of the grand old 5th Brigade struck up its marching air on the first step to Anzac. It seemed as if some hidden electric mechanism of the body were all at once athrill and aflame. Again it came as we in our turn got the word for war, took a thoughtful turn when approaching Lemnos officers were served out ball cartridges for revolvers. The wounded, whom we met by the way, were so candid in divining fate. 'Good luck! It won't last long, boys. You'll be dead or knocked out in a few days.'

Next the tense suppression as, clustered upon the barges,

we stole in by light for Anzac Cove, with the sniper bullets cutting the water about us, zipping, and tearing upon the barge. When they came very close, everyone had the conviction that this particular bullet just missed him. With almost equal suddenness we realised the battle smell, that hanging vapour which in still weather is a pall about a war front, the haze with acrid odours of explosives mingles with the staleness of man-packed trenches. The guide who waited for us on the beach gave us the new chum's welcome. 'This gully is swarming with snipers on both sides,' said the malignant wretch. 'Make haste and make no noise.' He was flying light in the brief shorts of Gallipoli, and led a weary column, in heavy accoutrements and packs, a nice dance through the night to keep up with the Will o' the Wisp. Perspiration streamed from us, the moment we halted every man dropped from exhaustion, yet that gully was perhaps the safest path on Gallipoli. Then again came sense of imminent touch with it when Colonel Knox began his first conference with the cheering assurance. 'Gentlemen, we're in the consommé; but you've just got to stick it and play the game.' Personally I smiled, because of the beginner's supreme confidence that he at least is immune. So when the bomb marked for me came in due course the first quick thought was, 'It isn't impossible after all.' The first fitting of gas masks as we approached a later war zone brought another sudden flash of realism.

The over-strained, over-wrought man in battle generally has a feeling that every hate and offense is directed against him, personally and particularly. In one way it is a good thing, because it gives him a personal grievance, generates a fierce resentment, but it has its dangers. On one such occasion, with a great assault momentarily threatened, I heard the repeated order to 'Pass machine guns to the right' and hurrying down to ascertain the reason for it, found half-a-dozen quick-firers massed at a particular point and other parts of the trench stripped bare. Someone, 'with the wind up', had seen hordes of imaginary Huns threatening his own particular corner and, being wholly unstrung, had passed the word on his own impulse. As a matter of fact that great enemy assault never materialised. In observation we had at the moment absolute command of the situation. Overhead our planes had established their mastery. Now and again the enemy tried to send aloft an observation balloon, but the moment it rose our flyers dashed for it, like eagles for their game, and it was pulled hurriedly down or burst into flames. In a depression behind their line the Germans had massed for the great assault, but a shower of bombs from our trench mortars fell upon them, smashed up their formation, and suddenly relaxed their fighting face.

How different is the attitude to an ever present danger, the dash upon an enemy position bristling with the dominant machine gun. Almost everyone has that comforting conviction that his, at any rate, is a return ticket. The persiflage may spin out a little thin at times, but with the warp of solemnity is ever interwoven the woof of wit. 'If you don't happen to want them anymore, can I have your new boots?' Then a note of mock complaint in: 'Ain't you got nothing to bequeath to me, Bill?' Men are actually betting on casualties.

'Are you there, Scotty?'

'Yes, what do you want?'

'Only askin' you not to take too much care of yourself. You're the skinter in my book.'

The worst trial of battle is not always in the battle. At the second battle of Pozières, I had control of a carrying party to serve the line with ammunition and supplies, and ever between us and our objective was the enemy barrage, that hell-broth of bursting rending metal, half-veiled in earth and smoke. Men heavily laden ran that gauntlet as often as six times a day, men who worked to the last minim of their energy, until they fell exhausted and slept actually in the curtain of death. So, in a few days of heroic effort, our numbers were considerably lessened.

There is little time for mourning in or after battle; the time for long, sad thoughts come much later when memory counts over her hallowed recollections. What a gallery of lost heroes in the cost and casualties of such a fight at Pozières: men who went out before their time; the picked prey of fate and circumstance. Amongst the unforgettable ones, with whom to have campaigned for even a little time was a life's privilege, were Major Eric Brind, who led the attack of the 23rd Battalion, Major Murdoch McKay and Captain Herbert Curnow of the 22nd Battalion, grand spirits with much of that fine chivalry, that exalted courage in their nature, which we are too apt to associate only with great worthies of their past. Major Brind with seen lying wounded in the battle zone, and in an obliterating burst of shell passed out of being and one of sight forever. Bracketed with them in fondest recollection are others like Captain Arthur Kennedy, who fell wounded near the German lines, was taken prisoner and died afterwards in Germany. In his case the Hun seemed to have acted decently, for they sent all particulars of his end to his wife, with a photograph of his grave.[15]

The distinction as between courage and unconsciousness of fear is a hackneyed topic. The man of high courage in its moral meaning is generally the man of vivid imagination and a full realisation of fear. The one suffers acutely and only his pride, his moral courage, carries him successfully through the strain. The other, much more rare, is the man who is unconscious of physical fear, and he is usually a man of dulled imagination. One takes risks for a definite end, drives himself to do the big thing, because it will be a gain to his side; the other takes risks which have no military value after all.

Another of the queer contradictions of battle strain is that men who had survived all the earlier terrors of assault and bombardment, reached the state of hanging on doggedly day after day, go to pieces as soon as relief is promised them. It may be because of the ever changing exigencies of battle, or for some purpose which personally I am unable to appreciate, but relief seldom came when it was first promised, postponement became known in trench language as 'the relieving stunt.' With the prospect of early relief men become intensely careful; their disappointment over delay finds angry and impatient expression. When relief comes, however tired men may be, there is an immediate rush for safety, with sometimes bitterly ironical happenings before the succour and rest of the far back billets are reached. The whole 'ordeal of battle' is a text of strange sermons that have rarely been preached, a phrase of profound and mysterious meaning.

Chapter 7

Men and episodes

In a record of personal impression I shall not dwell at any length on those hard, undecided earlier battles by the Somme (Armentières and the first and second battles of Pozières) which, with the Gallipoli landing, the Lone Pine endeavour, and last and greatest of all, the immortal turning point at Amiens, are the milestones on the Anzac march. History will deal with these in more calmly considered fashion through the years to come, when the secrets of strategy and purpose are laid bare, and even those who fought the fiercest of these struggles may, for the first time, realise just what they were trying to do. I was still with the 23rd Battalion when the first Pozières battle was fought, and had transferred to the 22nd when the Old German Lines were attacked a second time.

In neither case was easy right of way offered. In the first attack the 23rd had about five hundred casualties. When the turn for the 22nd came their later losses were heavier than those of any battalion on the Somme—800 men and 32 officers in a strength of 1100, including reinforcements. The losses were sustained less in the actual storming of Hun positions than in hanging on to them under a grimly Niagara of shells.

In these fights one had acquaintance with several battalion commanders whom it was an honour to serve. Amongst them was Colonel William Brazenor who was the Adjutant of the 71st Citizen Regiment when I served in that Ballarat unit. He became Colonel and Commanding officer of the 23rd Battalion, acted often as Brigadier and won the DSO and Bar. He won also the confidence of his men, at the very outset, in two qualities which have ever commandeered the respect of Australian soldiers—cool courage in action and absolute justice in all things. No better example could be cited to confound that heresy so popular with civilians—which still dies hard—that the preparations of peace time had been of little value in war where the unexpected, the unforseen, became the rule of operations. Colonel Brazenor started as a text book soldier, one who knew the theory and technique of his job outright. In the essentials a strict disciplinarian, in trifles a wise ruler, everything that he had learned in peace training was afterwards a gain to his command.

Lieutenant Colonel George Morton and Major Matthew Baird, two other Ballarat officers much admired, had the bad luck to be passed out, the first-named from Egypt, the latter at Gallipoli. Another distinguished leader was Colonel Wilfred Fethers, whose gifts in outright candour and clear expression made it impossible for anyone to misunderstand his meaning, especially his censure, just as his fine personality commanded always loyal obedience. He was knocked out at Pozières, so lost to a battalion which valued him.

Brigadier General Robert Smith, whose decorations include the DSO and CMG was another leader of the resolute type, and led the battalion with distinction at Bois Grenier, Armentières, Pozières, Ypres and other fighting sectors. He was above all things a sticker, with determination and will power developed to the highest degree, very severe on defaulters behind the line, but an inspiring leader in front of it. That is where he came by most of his honours and his nickname 'Fighting Bob'. He had a fertile mind for any ruse likely to embarrass the enemy. At Bois Grenier there was a gramophone in the first trench, and the CO one night suggested putting on a couple of records to interest the enemy, for the lines were very close just there. The Huns applauded and shouted encore. 'Give them another,' said Colonel Smith. Again the enemy applauded, but the encore this time was a sudden burst of fire from the machine guns which had been carefully trained on his parapet beforehand in correct anticipation of actual happenings.

Brigadier General Charles Brand, CMG, DSO, wounded in the South African campaign, was another who duplicated in the first degree the qualities of soldier and gentleman—game, genuine, genial. Colonel Aubrey Wiltshire, MC, DSO, Captain and Adjutant of the 22nd Battalion on Gallipoli, and who had the good fortune to see it through with the corps, was another soldier who learned his lesson in peace and applied it quietly but thoroughly in war. He won his way up when yet very young, was for months in command of a battalion without the rank of Lieutenant Colonel, because at twenty-six he was considered too young for the seniority. Those who knew and served with him had, however, no doubts on that point. As he lay wounded at Pozières my batman, Jones, wished to bring him in, but was told to take a wounded private first. 'And don't swear like that, Jones,' the Colonel added. It made an impression. 'He's a good man,' explained Jones to his mates, 'and if he says it's not right to swear, then it isn't right, and I'm knocking off.'

Until he left the field disabled, the 23rd had a very efficient commander in Lieutenant Colonel George Knox, CMG, who in his second baptism—that informal christening by the ranks—became, entirely without reproach, 'Nobby Knox'. He too had citizen training with the Scottish regiment before the war.

Never was the union of the churches more completely achieved than in the happy chaplain-companion of Chaplain Albert Bladen of the 23rd Battalion and Chaplain Edward Goidanich of the 24th Battalion, both of whom did so much for the spirit and comfort of the troops in the darkest days at Gallipoli and along the Somme. One was a Wesleyan, the other a Roman Catholic; men of different faiths but exactly the same immortal type—helpful in difficulties, comforting in sorrow, perennially cheerful in periods of peace. They jibed at, joked with and thoroughly understood each other. Everyone loved the two cheerful padres, the two constant pals. In their example, their character, their splendid attitude in all circumstances, hundreds gained a new conception of religion that, without profession perhaps, will yet influence them through life. Chaplain Goidanich got his DSO; Chaplain Bladen won it many a time—all the time. Once as he read the burial service by a soldier's grave at Gallipoli, a Turkish shell found the quiet hollow and burst close to him. The mourners ducked for shelter. When the smoke cleared the brave old Padre alone stood erect, unshaken, no tremor in the solemn words, 'Ashes to ashes; dust to dust.' When his time expired Chaplain Bladen refused to go home, preferring to be with the lads he loved and served so well to the end.

I have often been asked about the Australian point of view in those striving days around and after Pozières, when the pendulum of battle showed no particular bias. As to the possibilities of war, it may be illustrated briefly. When rations were abundant, supply certain, we were winning the war; when they were short we were losing it, but all felt that it would all be a matter of years. Comparisons between France and Gallipoli were frequently made, and, summing up considerations, the decision was, 'Better six months of

France than six weeks of Gallipoli.' It was a just estimate. In spite of the greater perfection of the German mechanism for war, the Australians soon realised that they were morally his masters. There was nothing of brag in the belief that in close combat one Anzac was as good as two Huns, for time and again they proved it. On anything like equal terms the Bosche always flinched from the test of the bayonet. Their moral had been established in dependence upon the power of multitudes rather than of men. Neither in character or courage have they any regard for our sporting maxim 'man to man'. The mass is everything, the unit little. In initiative the Australian was surpassed by no other troops fighting in Europe; his weakness was want of self-restraint. In the one quality he represented the maximum, in the other—almost equally important— the minimum, and, though with experience came a greater self-restraint, we paid for it heavily in casualties, bought with much of our best life-blood.

Amongst civilians in Australia one finds a sort of pride in the impression that their fighting men were undisciplined, and that it didn't really matter. Both impressions are utterly wrong. Only boys or weak headed men hold glory in that belief now. The tendency to make a cheap hero of the man who despised discipline did much harm in Egypt, but that error, scorched at Gallipoli, was killed outright in France. The fact is that in the essentials of discipline, absolute obedience in battle, the end at which all the ridiculed formalities of peace time aim, the Australian had no superior. He not only possessed discipline, but was proud of possessing it. An officer who had proved himself in the only way that counts could rely upon his men for implicit obedience, even command that outward show of respect which no thinking leader greatly values for its own sake, rather as the symbol and indicator of that disciplinary method and understanding which is so very important in action. The salute, for example, is a favourite subject either for a joke or a jibe, but like almost every other ceremonious detail there is a material purpose behind it which the civilian does not always grasp. Of all illusions that flourish best when transplanted, this one about discipline—a hardy annual in Australia, a noxious weed that was soon cut down in France—was furthest from reality. War is the great school of self-discipline—there, only, may the uncertain come to know themselves.

The realisation that one has nerves as well as muscles comes to most men in a campaign where the stunts follow each other in fairly rapid succession, and is always an unpleasant discovery. The unsettling suspicion that I was taking rather too much care of myself became, at about this time, an unhappy obsession. I found myself ducking to them occasionally, getting little jumps from shells bursting much too far away to be really dangerous. The natural antidote for that ailment is a short rest, though one cannot always get leave just at the moment he most needs it, and possibly in that way many misunderstandings have occurred. If it were only possible to cultivate perfect candour, the sensible thing would be to see the Commanding Officer and explain but, just when your nerves are punishing you, is about the last moment you would choose for such a confession. I was in a support trench at the time about three hundred yards behind the line, and, what mattered most of all, in charge mainly of reinforcements. It would never do for men new to the front line to get the impression that an officer was funking. A man may fool himself, but he will not fool the quick intelligence surrounding him, by whose conclusions he is made or damned.

Having occasion to go up to the front line, I decided, in no spirit of heroics, but as the plain way of testing myself, to walk across the open instead of following the communication trench, so in a conspicuous Sam Brown belt—which was never worn up the line—and swinging a swagger cane, I started across feeling sure that I would be sniped *en route*. I had a couple of close shaves, but, in reinstating self-confidence, the experiment was quite satisfactory. Hauled before headquarters for this indiscretion, any reason was given, of course, except the right one. Later on, at Les Boeuf, I was carpeted for indiscretion a second time. The Bosche patrols were very busy just then. Their snipers used to creep up at night within a hundred and fifty yards of our line. While one fired a pistol flare to light up the parapets, the others got ready to snipe anyone they happened to surprise outside the trench. It was exasperating, so Jones and I rushed out at a favourable opportunity with the idea of getting behind them for a shot. It came off. One of the Bosche, whom I could just see on the sky line, walked boldly right into the glare, and though the first shot missed, the second crumpled him up. Someone must have talked, for again there was a lecture.

I saw the perpetual battle between will and nerve fought out to a magnificent finish in the case of Lieutenant Walter Filmer, 22nd Battalion, who had been my senior in the City of Ballarat Battalion at home and, like many more, had to sink his rank before he was accepted for service. He came first to the Western Front in October 1916, when the season and trenches were at their worst—mud, cold and a concentration of all the miseries. He had become a Sergeant Major in Egypt and got to Ypres as we were about to take over Sanctuary Wood, so on the night before I took him for his first view of the front trenches. They were the worst I had seen, inundated with water, clogged with mud, and as we trudged along the gutter that was to be our happy home next day, Filmer asked, 'Where's the front line?'

'You're in it now,' I explained, and he was silent for a long time, thinking.

As we went back across the open the Huns were searching the roadways with machine guns and got a burst very close to us. Several bullets passed between us, one went under my foot. Filmer insisted that I was hit, and was not content until he had run his hands over my back to make sure. I could see that he was rattled. I was not surprised when, a few nights later, he asked my permission to go out with the scouts, explaining candidly that he wished to prove himself. So he was sent on wiring and bombing excursions, later went out alone, and so found himself again. He was killed at Bullecourt, having won the reputation of being the most courageous of a company which had amply proved its daring, an epitaph hard to win. While carrying Stokes shells up to the line he was wounded and told to go back. 'Oh no,' he said, 'they must have the shells,' so he struggled up again just as the Germans in a counter attack almost annihilated the wasted company, and there severely wounded a second time, Filmer fell and was never seen again.

The ironies of war have seldom been more happily pointed that in an incident on the Somme. Companies had been instructed to send night patrols into no man's land, but one company commander, mistaking the order, sent out his whole strength, and moving round at night I suddenly discovered that a section of trench was empty, and my own flank in the air. A whole company had vanished and no one knew where. The Commanding Officer delivered himself on the subject with incisive eloquence, and his vocabulary was exceptionally fine. Upon him was the responsibility, and he was for the moment in despair. Just then the Hun batteries opened a surprise bombardment of our trench, and it continued for some time with exceptional fury. No part of the line was so heavily battered as the section which should have been held by the lost company, which sitting out safely in the darkness heard the iron torrent tearing overhead. Before nightfall the report came that the company had reoccupied the trench without casualties.

'By Heavens, I've got it!' explained the CO, 'It's nothing short of inspiration,' and he wrote: 'This officer, acting on his own initiative, took his company out into no man's land, and so escaped the heavy fire which the enemy laid upon his trench soon afterwards.' The immediate result was a Military Cross, and never were the congratulations offered by comrades more genuine. As Shakespeare said, 'Our indiscretions oft do serve us well, when our deep plots do fail.' The man who had missed his decoration in many good things, and won it in his only mistake, was the very best of fellows.

The German sense of humour was illustrated in an incident at Fleurbaix about the time the first Zeppelin was brought down in England. With canvas and wire we made a very good imitation of a model airship, and labelling it with the number of the lost Zeppelin, carried it out one night and suspended it to a tree in no man's land. As soon as it was light the Bosche saw the model and the point, and did not rest until he had strafed it with machine-gun fire.

Chapter 8

A daylight adventure

On the night of our raid the company was due for relief, but with the change in circumstances two days later found us carrying on and pretty well knocked out from fatigue. We were still uncertain as to the actual position of the enemy, but since we were under machine gun as well as shell fire, it was quite evident that he was not far distant. As there was urgent need for more positive information, I received orders to send out an officer's patrol for a daylight reconnaissance and more definite news. With a spell of duty extending beyond ordinary limits, and the strain of a night raid added, the company officers were by that time so completely knocked out that I hesitated about asking any of them to undertake this duty, so decided to go myself, taking only my batman, Private Sydney Shearn, with me. For a while the contour of the ground gave us protection, and coming upon an old communication trench about two feet six inches deep, and leading obliquely from our lines in enemy direction, we decided to crawl down the trench as far as possible. It was not a pleasant place for a crawl, as the bottom was an indefinite depth of soft slimy mud.

After following the trench for some distance, it occurred to me that bluff, in the circumstances, was a better ruse than concealment, for the chance of being able to reconnoitre their position to any advantage in full daylight was remote. With better knowledge of the casual trench than we possessed, the enemy was not likely to overlook its possibilities. The better plan, it seemed to me, was to drop all pretence of concealment, show ourselves boldly, and walk towards them across the open. When audacity may be mistaken for sheer stupidity it is often more useful than extreme caution.

In a fold of the ground we left the trench, and immediately upon crossing the ridge we were surprised to meet a Highland officer. I asked him what he was doing out there alone, and in a Scottish accent quite thick enough to be convincing, he explained that he belonged to the Scots Brigade who were on the left of the Australians, that he had got mixed up as to his locality, and wished to know just where he was. It was only the remarkable circumstance of coming upon in out there in no man's land that made me suspicious.

'Where are you going?' he asked. I explained and he replied. 'Oh, you are making for Gamp and Malt Trench. You're aware, I suppose, that our fellows bombed it down and captured it last night? They're in possession of it now.'

'It's very strange,' I pointed out, 'that we should have no information about it. Are you sure you're making no mistake about the trench?'

'No mistake at all,' he said. 'It is a wonder you were not informed. Go over and see for yourself—you'll find our fellows there all right.'

The fact that he admitted being mixed up as to his own whereabouts convinced me that he was mistaken about Malt and Gamp Trench, although there was nothing else in his features, conduct, speech or dress, to excite suspicion or suggest that both of us were at that moment engaged in exactly the same game—bluffing the enemy into the belief that we were a pair of lost sheep, and the Hun likes to 'catch 'em alive' when opportunity offers. I was gambling wholly on that theory. He was increasing his protection, yet doubling his risk in wearing our uniform, for if captured meant sudden death.

The spy who accepts your hospitality in peace time to get information which he will use against your country in war, represents a form of espionage that may be desirable. But the military spy who enters your ranks, wearing your uniform, trusting wholly to his own nerves and mental resources to deceive you and dodge death, is another affair altogether. Discovery means short shrift for a long journey. It was a notorious fact that many of their most daring and successful spies were Austrians, possibly because in features and speech they were better fitted for the enterprise than the Prussian. A German in Scottish uniform, and with an unimpeachable Scottish accent, seemed such an utter absurdity that I could, although still uneasy, find no further excuse for questioning him, though in directing him on his way I was careful to give him directions that would land him at our headquarters instead of the place which he professed a wish to reach.

Moving on across the open it was soon clear that trenches in front were occupied, as we noticed groups of two or three men about seven hundred yards away on our right front. Shearn wished to get down and snipe at them, but I refused to let him as there was still a possibility that the Scottish officer was correct. It was at least a case in which 'better to be sure than sorry' held good.

We came within three hundred yards, and could quite clearly make out the line at the junction of Gamp and Malt Trench, with very strong entanglement on *our* side of it. If the Scots had taken it, they were very slow in reversing the parados and parapet, and getting their protective wire in the spot where it could do most good. Suspicion strengthened again, and as we moved I took quick mental note of every detail of significance. Just then a party of about sixty or eighty men in kilts got out of the trench on the further side, walked openly along the parados for a chain or so, and dipped down out of sight again. It looked like a fatigue party going to or leaving work.

'A dashed good job you didn't fire,' I said. 'They are Scots all right,' and the lad agreed.

In spite of the kilts and all convincing detail, some suspicion still lingered. 'Go slow—lest you halt forever!' was the warning from within. The old shelter trench was still close by, so I told Shearn to lie down in it and keep a sharp look out while I went on. When near enough to be easily heard I called out, 'Who are you?'

There was no reply, but one of the kilties beckoned me on. Again I called out. Still no answer but the beckoning arm. Lest the voice should not have carried I semaphored with my arms, 'Who are you?' Once more they beckoned silently.

'Do you think you can find your way back to headquarters?' I asked Shearn.

'No,' he said, 'I don't think I can.'

Holding my rifle up in the air, and then throwing it ostentatiously out of reach, I in turn beckoned for someone to come forward from the trench and meet me. In reply a soldier, not in kilts, but wearing some drab uniform quite unlike the German field dress, stepped out of the trench and came slowly forward and I advanced to meet him. We were about seventy yards apart, and within a hundred and twenty yards of their wire, when a warning shout came from Shearn lying in the trench beside me.

'Look out, Sir,' he called. 'There are men coming out on both flanks.'

A glance to either side showed me that the time had come for quick thinking. Two men, carrying rifles and unmistakably in German uniforms, were moving out on either side, evidently with the intention of getting behind and cutting me off. At the same instant the muzzles of about sixty rifles showed over the lip of the trench, all aimed straight at me. It was a very tight corner, and the Hun must have flattered himself that he had both in the bag.

Knowing that on the first sign of flight they would fire, and that I could not hope to get very far, I wheeled suddenly and made a dash for life, diving head first into a handy shell hole about thirty yards away. I had barely touched bottom when about thirty bullets flicked the mud all about it. Calculating quickly the time lost in working the bolts of their rifles, I dashed a little further for another shell hole. They were fortunately numerous. Again I just managed to beat their fire, and with a third dash I was into the trench alongside Shearn, landing in about six inches of soft slimy mud.

Had the Huns only known it, we were at their mercy, for our rifles were so choked with mud while dragging through the trench as to be quite useless, and the Bosche riflemen on the flanks were still coming on.

'We can't stop them,' I said to Shearn. 'Cut for your life and drop every ten yards.'

So in dashing and dropping, always under their fire, we dodged our way across six hundred yards of open ground to the shelter of one of those sunken military roads, so common in that part of France, roads which had been made for the services of peace as well as war, and sunken so that armies using them may be under cover. Readers of history will remember that more than a hundred years ago just such another sunken road was a factor in the tactical movements of Waterloo.

I saw and heard no more of the Scottish officer, whose gift of tongues was quite clearly not shared by anyone else in their line. He must have chuckled inwardly when I gave him wrong directions, for he obviously knew just as much about the location of our troops as his own. In spite of the mortification of having been successfully bluffed, I can even now admire his complete self-possession, his unusual gifts as a linguist. He probably watched the whole play from the shelter of a shell hole, and prudently lay low when, contrary to all reasonable expectations, we got back safely. I kept an eye lifting for the Scottish officer, for there could have been no more satisfactory ending to that exciting afternoon patrol than the pleasure of stalking and killing him.

Passing down the trench later in the day I overheard Shearn giving his mates a vivid account of the adventure.

'And I tell you one thing,' he added decisively. 'I'm not going to be his batman any more. I might have known that he'd take me out on one of his silly stunts.'[16]

It seemed to be an episode happily ended, but, if true in peace, it is doubly so in war that, 'the night cometh which no man knoweth.'

Chapter 9

The last stunt

The report of that lively reconnaissance had just been written when word came from the Commanding Officer that he had received a message from headquarters, instructing him to attack Malt and Gamp Trench at nightfall.

'What about artillery preparation?' I asked.

'There will be none,' he explained.

'And no artillery support?'

'Not a shell!'

I told him what I knew of the trench, how strongly it was held, how impossible, without artillery preparation, against its strong entanglements.

'It doesn't matter,' he said. 'We've got to do it. But you

must not go over. You've had a solid go already. An officer in reserve will take over the attack.'

'It will be very hard on the boys, Sir,' I urged. 'Tell them it's quite impossible to get through. It's a useless, hopeless stunt.'

'What am I to do?'

'Ring up Brigade, Sir, tell them of my reconnaissance, and ask them for artillery preparation to beat down the wires.'

The reply was that no artillery aid was possible, that the attack must go on at all costs. I never had a doubt as to the result. The attack might be heroic, but it was hopeless, and in the conjunction of these two words in war is the whole gamut of tragedy. 'Well, Cull,' said the C.O. 'I'm sorry to ask it, but you know the ground; you had better lead the two companies.'

By that time I was in no condition to lead a desperate venture. With six days and nights in the trenches, very little sleep, and for the last forty-eight hours scarcely anything to eat, I was just upon the point of collapse from fatigue— in anything by the condition for 'a forlorn hope'. In all the circumstances some sense of depression might have been expected. Premonitions were being discredited, almost every day, yet still persisted. Knowing absolutely all the difficulties of this duty, confident that few of us could escape its consequences, I had the most profound conviction that I would personally return unscathed. But my mind was full of gloom, my heart of grief for the gallant company who were to go upon a quest where valour within the limits of human possibilities as of little avail. The companionship of battle makes one very tolerant as to little indiscretions, appreciative of great virtues. And my boys, who possessed in high perfection some of the finest attributes of manhood, were to be sacrificed!

'Can't you get round their wires?' asked the commanding officer. The question showed that he too realised the hopelessness of getting through them, yet had no real appreciation of the position and could have none, unless he could see those triple lines of continuous entanglements as I had seen them. We were to rendezvous in the sunken road, which for a second time that day furnished refuge. There was still light enough, as we marched down, for the Germans to see us and put an intense artillery barrage over the spot, though fortunately we were well under shelter before they laid it down. There we waited some time for the troops which were to co-operate with us, but none arrived. With a full sense of my responsibility to the men whom I was to lead to sure destruction, I took advantage of those few moments to send a last appeal to the second-in-command.

'In view of the fact that units supposed to co-operate have not materialised, and that the Huns are putting down a heavy barrage—guns and machine guns—may we, not even now, have artillery support?'

The reply was curt and conclusive.

'Attack at all costs.'

It was an order so definite, received an hour after the time originally fixed for the assault, that there was no alternative but to carry it through, comforting oneself with the belief that behind the sacrifice was some hidden reason such as that which influenced our move against the Butte de Warlencourt a few nights before.[17] The luck of that hazard too stimulated the hope that, even without the element of surprise, I might still chance to find some lane through the German entanglements large enough to pass a few men at a time. Scouts were sent forward to feel for such an opening, but no news came back. Hope that such passage might exist, I had conformed the attack so as to have a better chance of finding and making use of it. Instead of advancing in waves—a plan by means of which, with the wires beaten down by gun-fire, casualties were lessened—we moved in column of shallow sections, roughly single file at intervals, a method afterwards adopted, I understand, at Bullecourt for an advance against machine-gun nests or 'block houses.'

It was so dark that for a time we advanced unobserved and without casualties, until within sixty yards of the wire. And such a barrier! Forty yards of almost solid wire, with slight intervals breaking it into distinct bands—a barbed breastwork some four feet six inches in height. Even in broad daylight and without any opposition it would have been difficult, but to break a path through such a barrier against a strongly protected enemy, with machine guns each firing 600 rounds a minute, the utter hopelessness of it may be realised.

A last halt in the shell holes, in hope that the scouts might still return with some news of import, and, while still lying on the ground, I shouted the order to charge.

Once under their flares we were as fully exposed as in daylight, and immediately the deadly shower of bomb and bullet struck us. From that point it was just a maddening melee—pure martyrdom, with doomed but dauntless men tearing hopelessly at that impregnable wire with bare and bleeding hands. There was but one idea—to get as far forward as we could, and use our bombs.

The impetus of the rush carried me right over the first barrier so that I fell in the open space between. The next effort found me in their second layer of wire, hopelessly entangled and held. Bombs were bursting so close that the flame almost reached me. I had just thrown the second last of my own bombs when one of theirs fell right under me, the force of the explosion blowing me clean out of the detaining wire into the open space again. I remember calling out: 'God! My hip's smashed.'

I tried to move and crawl out, but my body seemed to be paralysed, my legs were quite useless, life and the power of motion remained in my arms alone. Lieutenant William Corne and Private Claude Martin both heard me call, and were soon alongside.

'It's all right, Captain, we'll get you out.' One of them held up the wires while the other tried to drag me under, but I was still fast. Looking along the line, everywhere as bright as day under the Hun flares, it seemed most of my poor fellows were hanging and struggling in the wires. Some had fallen limply forward and ceased to struggle. Everywhere was the cry: 'Pass the word for stretcher-bearers,' but none came. They too had been knocked out.

I told Lieutenant Corne, a good and plucky officer, to go along the line and see what he could do. If nothing more was possible, he was to collect the men and take them back. Before he left Private Martin went down on his hands and knees and asked the Lieutenant to place us back to back, so that he could try and crawl out with me. But I had been partly disembowelled by the bomb explosion, and the moment Martin attempted to crawl I fell off helplessly.

'There's no chance,' I said, for I was a heavier man than Martin, and with 800 yards even to our outposts to go, I realised the impossibility of it. Corne had only moved about three paces away when he stepped right into a burst of machine-gun fire, and with a single exclamation fell dead. I asked Martin to put me into a shell hole, if there was one near, and to get away himself. Just then a machine-gun burst swept close to us. I saw the flash of a bullet as it struck their wire. With the velocity somewhat lessened, it caught me an angle blow across the forehead, and the blood for a moment blinded me. To my mind it was the finishing stroke.

'That's done it, anyhow,' I said. 'Just wipe the blood out of my eyes, drop me into a shell hole, and you get away.'

'Oh no, you'll be all right, Sir.'

'Yes, I'll be all right now. Nothing can do me any harm, so you must save yourself.'

'No, I'm going to stay with you, Captain,' he said emphatically. 'I won't leave you.' As he held me up he was sobbing like a child. Then he bent down and kissed me on the forehead. 'No, I won't leave you,' he persisted.

'Laddie,' I said, 'nothing can do me any more harm. If you stay you will be either captured or killed. It's your duty to go back.' So my last word to that true comrade was a command that he should retire. As he turned a few paces off, illuminated in the flares, I shall never forget the regard that shone in his brave, loyal face. In or out of the lines he was a dare-devil. Not that war, its pains and its sacrifices, matter at all to Martin now. He is waiting for the daybreak out yonder, one of the lost heroes.[18]

For a while I must have fainted. When I came back to consciousness it was still without pain, only a feeling of stunned helplessness, but with my vision still fairly clear. It was a horrible awakening. All around me men were groaning in their agony. I put my hand back to feel for my wounds, but there seemed to be nothing like a bloody pulp. I had shut my teeth hard with the determination not to scream, but in spite of it one groan, springing from the depths of utter misery, escaped me, and it seemed somehow to ease the pain which had suddenly become intense. With the thought of tetanus I kept my jaws working, wondered how long it would be before the end and whether the Germans would come out in time to take me alive. Now that there was no longer any hope of escape, I wished that they would come, though what the Battalion would think of me if they knew that I was taken prisoner worried me. The thought was so bitter that for a moment I cared little whether I lived or died. Even if the Huns treated me humanely, it was a terrible price to pay for life. Then came thoughts of home, of my people, what it would mean to them, and, grinding my teeth, I determined to live. There was still one Mills bomb in my pocket, and thinking that, if the enemy found it, they might be tempted to try it on me, I buried it in the mud. While Martin and Corne were trying to drag me out the lanyard of my revolver had caught in the wire, so unhooking the revolver, I threw it away into the wires.

For a little while later I must again have fallen unconscious, and next I heard voices speaking in German behind me. Where there had been men groaning to the left of me was now complete silence; on my right the wounded were still calling out. The thought struck me that perhaps the Germans had killed them, and some time afterwards I knew that I owed them no apology for that suspicion. Then men were stooping over me, and one of them asked in French, 'What are you?'

'Captain,' I answered. For a moment afterwards there was a discussion in German, some them apparently a bit excited. Next one of them got down on his knees and felt me over.

'Where is your revolver?' he asked, and I told him that I hadn't got one.

'Where is your watch?' was his next question. It was on my wrist, and, with the contents of my pockets, soon disappeared. My Sam Browne belt, which he next examined, had little interest for him, and he tossed it out into No Man's Land, but took my compass and another souvenir.

'Get up and go in,' he said, but I explained that I couldn't.

'What are your injuries then?' I told him as far as I knew. 'Oh, you can hop along on one leg,' he remarked. 'We'll lift you up.'

They raised me partly to my feet, but again I went out, and when consciousness returned I was alone, lying in a shell hole. Then I noticed immediately that there was no more groaning to my right. In about three minutes the party of Huns were back again, this time with a waterproof sheet, on which they placed me. So with my campaigning ended, hope gone, and it seemed but little of life left, I was carried into the enemy trench, prisoner of war.

Chapter 10

Held by the enemy

From the trench I was carried down steps into a deep dug-out and placed upon a sloping plank which rested on the lower steps. The first act of the Huns was to strip me of my clothing, one of them with great eagerness pulling off the heavy pair of riding boots that I wore. These seemed to please his fancy greatly. He looked them over, patting them approvingly, and then smiled at me as though in appreciation of a gift. Next they started to drag off my riding breeches, but the agony was so horrible that I asked them to cut down the seams. They did, possibly because what remained of them after the shell explosion was of little use for any purpose.

After returning from the scout of the previous day, I had neither time nor opportunity to get a change of socks.

Those I wore were full of holes, wet from dragging through the mud and slime, and the night was bitterly cold. I asked them to take off the wet socks, but they simply shook their heads. They took all my clothes, excepting a shirt. Doctors and attendants came flocking around to examine my wounds, and quite a number of their soldiers came down to have a look at the fallen enemy. On seeing the nature of the injuries some of their faces at least expressed pity, but there was one fellow who laughed, clapped his hands, and made no secret of his exultation. 'Most of them seem all right,' I thought, 'but save me from being left alone with that bird.' I couldn't forget the strange way in which my poor fellows had ceased to groan, impossible and horrible as the sinister suggestion seemed.

The surgeon who dressed my wounds spoke to some of the others, who shook their heads. One of their officers who spoke English then questioned me.

'We were waiting for you,' he said, 'and had a welcome ready, but you were late, and we feared we might be disappointed. However, everything came off all right. It was a pretty big attack, wasn't it?'

Believing that this particular view was one to be encouraged and that he would be almost sure to take the opposite of anything I told him as the real fact, I answered, 'Oh no, it was only a reconnaissance.'

'I see,' he said with a smile. 'It was the big attack that we expected, all right.'

Noting how seriously they regarded, I grinned up at them, and the one who spoke English asked: 'What are you smiling at?'

'I was just thinking how very ineffective your grenades are. If that had been a Mills bomb I would have been blown to fragments. Your old thing only bent me.'

He stared at me in amazement for a moment, then spoke a few words in German to a companion who also inspected me as curiously as if I were some unusual freak.

Placed on the ground sheet again, I was carried from the dug-out and dumped carelessly on the top of the trench. Then commenced a tour of torture across the open ground. The night was dark and bitterly cold, and occasionally the carriers dumped me down roughly for a rest. Apart from sheer fatigue, I had lost so much blood that I went out again, and for a time everything was blurred. I had a hazy impression of being placed upon a lorry or the truck of some light railway, then carried through a ruined village, much battered by gun fire, sometimes through gaping fissures in walls, until my bearers halted in front of a building which had somehow escaped the general destruction. I was very weak then, unable to speak above a whisper, and tortured with pain. Down a corridor of this building, and into a stuffy basement which seemed to be a hospital ward with beds set in tiers, cabin-fashion, one above the other, and dimly lit. Here I was again insensible for a while, and on recovery was taken to the operating theatre, and an anaesthetic stopped pain and trouble for a time. On coming round, an orderly, whose English was excellent, explained that as to the rent in my side, nothing could be done with the limp, hanging flaps of flesh, and these had been cut away. Again the balm of complete oblivion, and how long it lasted, I don't know.

On my struggling back to consciousness once again, the same orderly was standing by. He felt my pulse and shook his head. 'I can't feel it,' he said, then put his hand over my heart. 'I can't feel your heart beat. You are about done, and will die tonight.'

At intervals of about twenty minutes during the day he repeated his reassurance, 'You will die tonight' and I was so utterly weak that it seemed he was likely to be right. I put my hand over my heart and could find no beating. If it meant death, it would at least end the excruciating pain.

Then, all at once, in spite of my weakness and that utter indifference which seems to be a blessed provision to make death easy, I found myself 'biting into the bullet' again. That reiterated, 'You'll die tonight' roused me, perhaps, better than anything else could have done. I determined that, in as far as my will had power to control the matter, I would not die. Shutting my teeth against it I whispered over and over again, 'I won't die!'

The enemy surgeons came once more, and after a whispered conversation in German, called for stretcher bearers, who took me out of the ward across a courtyard to what seemed to be a large railway goods-shed, with a single bed in it, where some German soldiers were billeted at night. I found out afterwards that, when death was regarded as inevitable, it was their common practice to take the patient out of the ward so that others might not be disheartened or disturbed. The ward was one for the worst cases, generally men who had been badly wounded by our shell fire. Two or three died every day, but the beds were not long vacant. Altogether it was a ghastly place.

In this shed I was offered a draught, which I refused to take. Later I learned that this was another convention with the German surgeon—an overdose of morphia to anticipate the impending end. Though some may think it callous, the purpose is humane, just a quiet transfer for the poor soul who is 'passing West' from the light to the longer sleep. Instead of dying, I went quietly to sleep, waking towards morning with the sensation that my feet were afire. I used the good foot to shuffle the blankets off, and each time I succeeded a considerate German soldier came over and put them back again.

In the morning, very much to the astonishment of both surgeons and orderlies, I was still alive and feeling better, so they carried me back to the ward and put me to bed again. The orderly told me that the man in the next bed was an Australian officer, and I found that he was Lieutenant Ahnall of the 7th Brigade, who had been badly wounded by a bomb.[19]

'You will be Captain Cull of the 22nd Battalion,' he said.

'How do you know?' I whispered.

He explained that his unit had attacked Malt and Gamp Trench twenty-four hours later, and before going in he heard that I had been killed. Several parties, he explained, had been sent out after the raid to try and get me. Two stretcher-bearers stated that they had found me, but that I was dead. His men, too, had charged into the German wire only to be knocked out helplessly, and he assured me that he had actually seen the Huns killing the wounded with the butts of their rifles.

'I know,' he added, 'they did the same with your men.'

They had professedly kept the wounded officers as what they called 'souvenirs' but really with the hope of extracting information from them later on.

'How long have you been here?' Ahnall asked.

'About twenty-four hours,' I said, but the orderly corrected, 'He doesn't know that he was unconscious for nearly three days.'

The Germans were much interested in a gold identification disc which Lieutenant Ahnall wore, possibly a present from his family or friends. They used to take it frequently from his wrist to show it around, and seemed to think it wonderful that a soldier's disc should be made of pure gold. It gave them a new, and from the German point of view, an appealing interest in Australia.

Ahnall had been badly cut about with a bomb and died early next morning. He was constantly pleading for water and the attendants explained that it would be wrong to give him any, though they frequently moistened his lips with a wet sponge. At midnight he was calling for his mother.

After six days in that hospital, which I was told was just outside Bapaume, I was taken in an ambulance with German wounded to another hospital at Cambrai, and before leaving the orderly said: 'Well, we are not so bad as they say, are we? Did you expect to be killed?'

'Certainly not,' I said. 'We treat your wounded well and we expect the same thing from any honourable enemy.'

I was the only Britisher in hospital at Cambrai and my presence seemed to cause a sensation. Soldiers rushed about yelling, *'Engländer! Engländer!'* They shouted something at me in German which I could not understand. Then one who knew English came along and asked me my rank.

'That's very good for one so young,' he remarked, and seemed to become friendlier. Later the orderly who had grinned and shouted at me came along, and taking me by the hand, said, 'Captain, I apologise.' Even in the case of an enemy rank claims respect in Germany. He next brought along a surgeon, a fine looking man, who was most kind in his attention, turning me carefully over to examine the wounds, and being evidently anxious to cause as little suffering as possible. In this he was a marked exception, though I had thus far no cause to complain of unprofessional treatment.

Next morning a German sergeant major, a short, strongly built man with a manner more frank and open than is usual with the Hun, came to see me. He spoke sufficient English to enable us, with a smattering of French here and there, to understand one another fairly well. He was so amiable, so anxious to please, that I suspected a purpose behind it. He would sit beside my bed for an hour each day, turning over illustrated papers of the usual propaganda pattern, showing maps of England with a chain of U-boats all around it. If the purpose were to draw me on to confidences, I could not but admire the thoroughness with which he went about it. But following such a policy they hoped, no doubt, that with my great weakness I would become an easy victim.

'Are you really an Australian?' he asked.

'Yes,' I said, 'why do you ask?'

'Oh, Australians are said to be such big men, but you are not a big man, nor are the other prisoners we have taken lately big men.'

'Oh, that goes for nothing,' I explained. 'You see, in the smaller stunts of no importance Australian commanders only send over the weeds and keep all the big men in reserve to give you a towelling by and by.'

'Oh, you are splendid soldiers all right,' he admitted. 'You fight very bravely, but you cannot hope to beat us.'

He knew about the Referendum vote in Australia, and asked: 'Why should you fight for England? The good Australians have turned her down. They say that they have done enough, and they are working for Germany now.'

In some measure he was correct, though that kind were not usually called 'Good Australians'.

One day, after a long dissertation on the devastation of London by Zeppelins, the starvation of all England by U-boats, I said, 'I'll wager you don't really believe it.'

He looked at me a long time before answering, then very slowly and a bit sadly answered: 'No, I don't believe it, but a great many of our people do.'

One item of news which he repeated over and over again was: 'You Australians have done enough for England. Since the Referendum they are afraid that you will be a trouble by and by, and the doctors take every opportunity of amputating when your men are wounded in the legs. They are sending crippled Australians by trainloads to Switzerland, 3000 of them. You can't hope to beat us. Time will show.'

'Yes, about two years!' I remarked.

'Two years!' he exclaimed in astonishment.

'Yes,' I said smiling. 'Don't you think you can last that long?'

Wounds, and especially the worst kind from shell or bomb, are not a pleasant subject to dwell upon in detail. It is sufficient to say that my wounds included the total loss of the right hip bone, thigh and pelvis both shattered, and the lower part of the abdominal wall on the right side torn away, so that I was partly disembowelled. There were many other injures, but that was enough. The mystery then and now, say the specialists, is how I managed to survive them.

Chapter 11

The devil and the deep sea

Wavering between life and death, and with the balance ever threatening to swing the wrong way, I still saw and realised sufficient to know that Germany was even then in serious straights for food. Even when they assured me boastfully that their U-boats were starving England, they knew by actual personal privation that their own case was desperately bad. For a morning meal they brought me a cup of acorn coffee and a hunk of black bread made from a mixture of rye, potatoes and wood pulp. At midday there was another cut of black bread with a watery vegetable soup—or by way of a chance a plate of sauerkraut or boiled carrots. Every second day I got a cup of cocoa or real coffee without milk or sugar.

One orderly, a little more considerate than the rest, asked if there was anything I wanted. I suggested that he might give me an injection with his hypodermic needle each night so that I might sleep and get relief from pain. He did so, but a few days later the surgeon explained that I could have no more morphia, as in my weakened state it would be sure to kill me. A couple of days later there was a second operation in which a large splinter of bone from the shattered thigh was removed. Just as I came out of the anaesthetic a German surgeon was bending over me, and in my half-delirium I swung a quick right handed blow, and fortunately for myself I just missed his nose, which was a very red one. For some days I was in a very low state and they pumped saline into the veins to make blood and keep me alive.

At about that time a new surgeon took over at the hospital, and proved to be one of the most absolute beasts whom I have ever encountered; a man with about as much humanity as one might expect in a Bengal tiger. His professional methods may have been correct, but he coupled with them the deliberate intention to torture. In cleaning the wounds he drew rough-cloth, see-saw fashion, back and forward through my side while I ground my teeth in agony and prayed that I might not gratify him with a groan. While probing the wounds he would look at me with a grin and ask, 'Does it hurt?' I could just manage to gasp, 'No,' though fully aware that such an answer meant more brutality.

In the next bed to me was a German soldier, who on the first morning that he saw this malignant beast dress my wounds turned sick. He waited until he was quite sure that the surgeon had left the ward, then looked towards me, said something in German and shook his head in a pitying way. Prior to that he had not noticed me, now he would nod to me in the morning, and whenever the surgeon came to dress my wounds this soldier used to put both his hands over his eyes so that he should not see the torture. With pus and blood the mattress of my bed had got into a horrible state. As it dried and hardened it was cutting into the flesh, and one morning with some reluctance I asked if the bed might be shaken out. The intellectual gentlemen flew into a rage, shook his fist in my face, and said: 'You swine-hound *Engländer*, it's good enough for you. You are lucky to be alive!' He was a particularly vile product of German Kultur.

After he had left the ward an orderly who could speak a little English whispered, 'Say nothing and I will fix it for you.' Four of them lifted me gently to the floor, furtively as if they were committing a crime. Keeping watch to see that the coast was clear, they brought a new mattress, explaining that I must keep silent about it or they would be punished for helping an *Engländer*. The orderly seemed to think that for the reputation of the hospital there was something owing to me, for that day he ransacked another man's kit, got a small parcel of sugar and brought it to me with the acorn coffee, remarking, 'You will be able to drink that stuff now.'

One morning there was a commotion in the hospital—
the orderlies rushing excitedly about shouting, '*Engländer!*
Engländer!' Some of our fliers over head—so near and yet
so far! My inquisitive friend, the Sergeant Major, after many
visits came at length to the point. One morning at about the
time when the British were taking over part of the former
French front, he came with a map and pointed out the lines
as they were now held. Having shown their own positions he
said carelessly: 'You have taken over from the French from
here,' with his finger on Ypres, 'right down to—let me see—
which side of Péronne does your line end?'

That was the vital question, and it had taken quite a lot of
clever camouflage to get to it. I looked at him, put my finger
across my lips, and smiled.

'Oh, I did not mean that,' he protested in quick
appreciation. 'I did not mean anything—I forgot. I am sorry.'

A few days later he came up for another try, but there was
'nothing doing'. His interest in the *Engländer* immediately
ceased.

Such distraction or entertainment as one might have had
in these incidents was overshadowed always by the positive
horror with which every morning I waited for the coming of
that surgeon. I used literally to sweat in apprehension, never
thought of him without a shudder. He was simply the last
possibility among human brutes; a man who, I am confident
really enjoyed the sight of suffering, a special and extraordinary
type even amongst a brutal people. For the mental attitude of

the German, even when he is not deliberately laying himself out for overbearing brutality, is, to say the least of it, peculiar. In the ward which I occupied was a German soldier who had become 'mental'. The antics of this poor demented wretch were a perpetual joy to the orderlies. They used absolutely to shriek with laughter over them. Once he tried to throw himself from a window, and, laughing still, they dragged him back to his bed, while patients who were not badly wounded joined in the mirth. The attempt at suicide was just the cream of the joke. I noticed, too, that even in dressing the wounds of their own soldiers there was little care used. Bandages were never eased off as they would have been in a British hospital. They were torn off quickly, possibly by order of surgeons who had their hands too full to waste time on mercy. Several of the wounded Germans in the ward tried to converse with me, and one youngster of about nineteen showed me with great pride a cake of toilet soap which his friends has sent him. Soap seemed to be a prize everywhere, that supplied to the hospital being made chiefly from sand. One day he passed me over his tin of jam and invited me to put some on my bread. Having neither money nor Red Cross supplies, the only luxury that came my way was an occasional bowl of barley broth.

Two ends of an incident are sometimes curiously connected. On the return to Australia I met one of my own lads who had also been wounded and taken prisoner in our last raid. He had been for some time in hospital at Cambrai, on the next floor above me, and mentioned one day that a German Sergeant Major had been very friendly and attentive.

'What was he like?' I asked.

He gave me a word-portrait of my cordial friend, the Pumper with the war map, which was so very faithful, so very entertaining in some little fancy touches that I enjoyed it thoroughly. The Sergeant Major had told him there was an 'Englishman' in hospital very badly wounded. 'He has no chance,' he used to explain. 'He must die tonight.' Next morning he would remark, 'Well, he didn't die last night, but they don't expect him to last through tonight.'

The next incident of interest was that I was to be taken away from Cambrai; whither I neither knew nor cared, having the strongest belief that, with that scourge of a surgeon at the head of it, there could be no worse torture chamber than Cambrai. With wider knowledge of Germany I might have been less sanguine, and the sufferings attacked to that transfer will neither be forgotten—nor forgiven.

It was March 15, 1917, still black winter in Germany and with snow falling, when I was taken with a number of German wounded by stretcher and hospital-train, or street-car to the railway station, where a hospital train was waiting. We were taken first to the platform where there was shelter, until casualty checks had been attached. Then the German wounded were immediately taken into the train and put to bed, but that was not my luck. I was taken along the permanent way close to the tail of the train, dumped into about three inches of snow, and left there. The only garment I wore was a cotton shirt, my only other covering a single blanket—chiefly cotton. A bitterly cold wind was blowing, and for nearly an hour I lay exposed to it. More than once I asked them to take me into the train. They merely grinned and passed on. There was no decent reason for not putting me under shelter at once. No reason that a white man could understand for taking me out of the shelter of the station into the snow. Finally two stretcher bearers, who, I had not previously seen, carried me into the train and told me to get to bed. As they spoke and understood English, I explained that my body was partly paralysed and that I could not possibly move. One of them gripped me by the back of the neck, the other by the legs, and pitched me into bed. It was just German cruelty and might have meant manslaughter.

For days I had been bandaged very tightly in order to stop the flow of blood. It was painful, but, as they explained, necessary. It seemed a pity to take trouble that might be wasted in a few seconds of careless or callous handling by stretcher bearers who were either ignorant or indifferent as to life or suffering.

As in all hospital trains the blanket had been placed in a roll at my feet, and with a grin they left it there. My body was blue from exposure; the cold almost numbed the pain. They watched me while I worked slowly, patiently and painfully with my left toe, trying to edge the blanket up within reach of my hand. Only one thing warmed me, pure, primitive resentful rage. There are many things which a prisoner in Germany's hands might desire. The one gift I would have taken in preference to all others then was just five minutes of my former life and strength, and those two Huns alone to share it with me. In the fighting line I had often lectured men of my own command who, because of something they had seen, or of which they had learned, vowed that they would never take another German prisoner. I had pointed out that an enemy, either wounded or prisoner was no longer an enemy, and that it would be murder to kill him. Many experiences in Germany helped to strengthen the point of view that the only good Hun is a dead Hun.

In that hospital train I met the first Red Cross nurse I had seen behind the German lines. She spoke such perfect English that for a moment I assumed that she was an English nurse who had been detained when war broke out.

'Are you English?' I asked.

'No,' she explained, 'but I was in England for some years.'

Not long enough, apparently, for reformation, because I found her afterwards German in every fibre, as coarsely indecent as the worst kind of German can be. The male of the species, if often efficient, is almost always brutal, but brutality is sometimes preferable to gross vulgarity, and my sincere wish afterwards was that I might not meet another German 'sister'.

On the second day I was taken into the operating car where about eight surgeons examined me. They seemed to be professionally interested in the wounds, some of them sympathetic, but one of them laughed and appeared to enjoy the spectacle of an enemy so badly mangled. 'You have something to suffer,' one of the surgeons said. 'Drink this,' and he offered me brandy. On my refusing he said, not unkindly, 'You must drink it, or I'll pour it down your throat.' They bandaged me very decently, and while doing it one of them put a cloth across my eyes and said, 'You must not see. It may make you down-hearted.' When I laughed they looked at me in wonder—they knew nothing of what I had seen and suffered at Cambrai.

That train-journey, with many interruptions, lasted for the greater part of three days, and they tried to make it as happy as possible with occasional sleeping draughts. At some of the stations where we halted women came into the train with biscuits and other comforts for the wounded. One of them was handing me some biscuits when an officer called out, '*Engländer!*' and after a moment's hesitation she passed on. On a second occasion, his warning was ignored. The lady called a companion who could speak English, and after a few kindly enquiries they gave me some biscuits. The journey ended at Bochum, which is not far from Essen in Westphalia, and I was taken by motor to St. Elizabeth's Hospital. In my recollection it was always be 'Black Bochum'.

Chapter 12

Still fighting

A few days after I reached Bochum an old soldier, one of the Diehards of that 'contemptible little army', was allowed to come and see me, but for some inexplicable reason his visits were immediately forbidden. It was a long time before I again saw or talked with any of my countrymen, through there were many of them in the hospital. One of the first visitors was a 'Tommy', an English lad, and I was deeply touched when, after his departure, I found upon the table a few marks which he had carelessly left behind, a very delicate and gentlemanly way of doing it. The first happy days I knew in captivity were when he was allowed to come to my room, where he washed, fed and looked after me like a brother.

Before leaving he brought a Belgian, who proved an equally good and constant friend. I shall never forget him. Originally he must have been a very fine type of physical manhood, almost perfection. In the first burst of the war he had been clubbed on the head with a rifle, and was still occasionally 'queer'. He hated the Bosche, and with reason, for his own family had been amongst the thousands of victims of their brutality. With tears in his eyes he told me that his brother's little girl, a child of twelve years, had been outraged by German soldiers. His wife was in occupied territory starving, his home had been destroyed, others of his relations murdered, but it was the tragedy of little Joan that drove him to fury. Should any of those insufferable beasts and assassins come in the big Belge's way there will, I feel sure, to be a stern account taken. He had then been a prisoner of war for about twenty months, eight of which he had spent in gaol for refusing to work in an ammunition factory. He had been in hospital some weeks before I met him, and was suffering from a badly scalded foot. Questioned as to the cause of it, he explained that, on refusing to work at munitions, a sentry with fixed bayonet was sent to force him, and in order to evade that duty he had deliberately turned a pot of boiling water over his own foot.

'I won't do it,' he said emphatically. 'Perhaps a bomb or a grenade that I am forced to make may kill my own comrades. If they make me go again I will cut three fingers off my right hand rather than help them win the war.' And that I felt sure that he would do it.

Such instances were not at all uncommon, both amongst French and Belgian as well as our own prisoners, and I was especially impressed with the heroism of one French soldier. Being forced to labour in a munitions factory, which he knew was against the covenant; he picked up a heavy billet of wood, handed it to a comrade and, holding out his arm, showed him where to strike so that the arm might be fractured. His friend hesitated, but, with his arm still stretched out, the brave chap turned away his head and shouted, '*Allez!*' The first blow failed in its purpose, and through screwed up with pain he again extended his arm with, '*Encore allez!*' I often wondered whether my own countrymen even faintly realised the fight that these great-hearted men were still making for conscience sake, what hardships and privations they suffered for the cause to which they had given themselves to the last extremity. Here in German prisons were thousands of silent sufferers still fighting the cause of Justice and Humanity, though many who hear of such instances outside were puzzled, and saw nothing in it but a foolish obstinacy.

On two occasions Australian prisoners from a *Lager* close by were permitted to visit me under escort, and once again I was given proof that, though their bodies had been captured, their spirit had not surrendered.[20] They were still fighting the Bosche with an ingenuity and determination which puzzled even while it exasperated him. Some of them were sent to sow a field with peas and beans, sentries being posted at one end of the plot. One man drew the drill, another followed closely, and apparently sowed the seed, a third covering it up. But not a single seed was dropped into the drill. The lot were dumped into a hold at the end of it, and when those peas grew it was the most amazing result in agriculture that a German farmer had ever known. The Hun is a good cultivator. His potato sets had been sprouted before they were handed to the prisoners, and, as they planted, every shoot was carefully snipped off. It was only when the peas came up that the Germans feared that the potatoes too might be a failure. It meant, of course, that the men were taken from the lighter work of the fields and sent to harder labour in coal mines. For trifling offences the usual punishment was being 'stood to the wires'. In winter or summer, hail or sun, they were compelled to stand in the open strictly to the German 'Attention' with Hun sentries to see that no one relaxed a muscle. The penalty for doing so was being clubbed with the butt of a rifle. If it happened to be winter they were lightly clad; in summer they were forced to stand bareheaded and facing the sun. The punishment continued until the prisoner either yielded or collapsed— when upon recovery it was continued.

I was greatly 'bucked up' by the visit of my countrymen, who on every occasion brought me packets selected from their Red Cross parcels—food, cigarettes, toilet necessaries, underclothing, all the things that were so very much desired. For weeks I had been ravenous with hunger, but refused to ask a favour. So wasted was my body that whenever my bed was made an attendant held me with his arms extended so that my injured side might not touch him, and he was no strong man. Never were the Christmas gifts of Santa Claus to a child a greater joy than those kindly gifts to me. Even to be with the splendid chaps who brought them, to see them and talk to them again, was both a physical and mental tonic. They must have wondered often at the excited eagerness with which I rummaged the boxes, my exclamations of delight as tinned sausages, biscuits, jam, soap, cigarettes appeared in turn. They were surprised to find that I had been so badly treated. 'We thought they gave officers more consideration,' said a Corporal, 'but we are better off than you.' Not better off than they deserved to be, for theirs is the most trying job on service, and the sequel to it was working for the enemy in coal mines, sugar refineries and on the roads.

Having on one occasion mentioned to the surgeon my belief that a broken bone in the wound was causing much of the trouble, he said: 'Pooh! You haven't a broken bone in your body. You will be playing tennis in about three months.' A few days later I saw the end of a bone splinter sticking out through the flesh, and feeling where my hip bone should have been could only find a hollow. 'Tennis in three months' was a playful form of German satire.

I was much worried by the fact that, as month after month passed, I heard nothing from home. Yet at Cambrai they had brought a card to me and held my hand while I signed the printed form: 'I am a prisoner in German hands—wounded.' Nearly four months passed before my people at home got that news. I had been ten months a prisoner before their first letter came.

Another Good Samaritan, as plucky as he had been unfortunate, who came to see me at Bochum was a young Scottish soldier. Poor fellow, he was in a bad way—had lost one foot through frost bite, while three toes were missing from the other foot, the heel bone of which had also decayed. He was able to get about fairly well on crutches, and coming every day brought me a share of each Red Cross parcel he received. As an example of 'No Surrender' his story is worth telling.

His battalion was on the Somme one night when a small detachment under a young officer were ordered to storm what was believed to be an isolated Hun post. They found it strongly defended and had a fierce fight. As long as their bombs lasted they held on against overpowering numbers. Their officer was wounded four times before he fell dead. Finally with only three men left alive, and each of them shot more than once, they decided to make a bolt for it. One was killed instantly, the others both brought down again wounded, but they got into shell holes and stayed there. It was the heart of winter, and they were soon crippled by the cold and frost bite. Their iron rations ran out. They ate grass, chewed their own papers, and so for eight days lived through intolerable suffering, only to be discovered and captured in the end by a German patrol. They were given hot coffee and sent at once to a German hospital where, with decent treatment, their feet might still have been saved. This poor chap was not done with suffering. Later both feet were amputated and he was finally repatriated. On leaving Bochum they took away his crutches, gave him a stick, hung his kit about his neck and ordered him to march. He was absolutely writhing, moaning in agony, but his brute captors only laughed and refused to allow any other prisoner to help him. Do you wonder that some of us who have seen and suffered these things until in time the agony and humiliation of it had burned into our very souls, have nothing to offer the Hun in future but a Hate as deadly as his own—no hand for him in the years to come, except in the form of a doubled fist!

Twice I was visited by padres, the first a fine type of a man who looked and spoke quite unlike a German, the second a typical Hun. Long afterwards, when I was able to sit in a chair, some Sisters of Mercy came and said that I must go to church—they would wheel me down. I had heard from French and Belgian prisoners that their services were just an appeal for the success of German arms, a plea for our downfall, and had no wish to say 'Amen' to such a prayer. For days the Sisters, none of whom could speak English, importuned me in French to go to their service. I felt that their purpose at least was genuine, and told them of my objections.

'Do you want me to pray, *Gott strafe England*?'

'No, no,' they said. 'All that is very wrong. This is just a Christian service, in which anyone may join.'

I hobbled down with the help of crutches, but was too weak to stand, and as no one wished apparently to make room for me, I had to come away or I would have fallen. If this is a fair sample of German piety it seemed to me lacking in some great principles of Christianity.

There were a few sisters about the hospital who attended chiefly to German wounded and had little to do with prisoners. Amongst the attendants were non-coms who occasionally came to my room, and one of whom was in a degree decent. He realised the seriousness of their economic position, and when there was no one to overhear admitted that almost everything was now 'Ersatz' (substitute). A cake of toilet soap, he explained, cost about six shillings. Pepper and salt were only for capitalists. He told a story of one German woman who had lost her bread card, and it took some time to replace it. She begged for bread for her children and was refused. Finally she stole a loaf, sent payment for it to the police and having divided the bread in four portions amongst her children, hanged herself to a rafter. Even then I realised that there was social unrest in Germany, a strong resentment against leaders who had brought them to such a pass, but I realised too the complete helplessness of any effective attempt at revolution. The civilian was too weak, too meek for anything like heroic reprisals, too completely overmastered by military method and power. The death rate, amongst the very old and very young especially, must have been abominable.

A boy was sometimes permitted to pass through the hospital selling picture post cards. He was only about twelve years of age and for the first time he played the game valiantly, 'Hoch *der Kaiser!'* and *'Gott strafe England!'* being part of his routine. They had plenty of food, he explained, were quite happy and sure to beat England. One morning, just after I had got my first Red Cross food parcel—four months after I had been taken prisoner—he came into the room, and when he saw the food on my table his eyes opened wide in astonishment. There was no *'Hoch der Kaiser!'* then. They were starving, he said—had nothing but soap and black bread. Would I sell him one tin of meat for his mother? One had to harden one's heart then, the boy's plea was so obviously genuine. With tears in his eyes he offered me every penny he possessed, but there was a principle which it would have been treason to ignore. Red Cross parcels were not yet being sent for the succour of those who had devastated the world, drenched Europe in blood.

It is hardly necessary to say here how beneficent the Red Cross attention to prisoners proved. It was their salvation, and because it saved German rations and made men fitter for work, the prisoners always got their parcels. There was at first some theft, but this was stopped when they placed armed guards in charge of the trains. One condition was that non-commissioned officers must always open and examine the parcels, and they had been so primed with news of the deprivation of the enemy that their wonderment over the contents of the parcel could not be concealed. The woollen clothing, especially the socks, puzzled them. One man, as he stretched a sock between his fingers said: 'It's wool all right.'

'Oh yes, it's wool,' I remarked. 'What is yours?'

Chapter 13

Dark days at Bochum

'Did you keep a diary?' many Australian friends have since asked. No diary is necessary to a wounded prisoner of war in Germany. Every little happening is indelibly stamped on the mind. 'Left is a chapter of small miseries which the philosopher plucks smilingly,' said a stoic. In Bochum life was a continuity of agonies mental and physical. If I ever smiled about them it was afterwards and over the wish that, when Germany was beaten, I could be military governor of Bochum for just one month. There is no difficulty in remembering. The Hun burns in his attentions as with vitriol.

I was taken to a small cheerless room, the only light in which came from a barred and frosted window. Alongside the wall was a heavy frame wooden bedstead. A small locker and a chair by the bedside was the only other furniture in this gloomy cell. On arrival I was taken first to the operating theatre by two German girls who appeared to be doing somewhat similar work to our VADs. They were about to lift me to the table, and I thought myself rather a hefty handful for two girls to manage, but was a little bit shocked when they made no more effort than with a featherweight.

One of my first acts at Bochum was to overcome as far as possible the consequences of a mistake. Just after the second operation at Cambrai I was visited by a German officer, apparently some high official, who asked questions as to my name, rank, battalion and division. A prisoner of war is not compelled to say to what division he belongs. The other details are necessary and compulsory. But, still muddled from the anaesthetic, the division slipped out. Getting hold of the papers afterwards I hid them under my shirt and, when opportunity offered, used an indelible pencil to rub out every trace of that indiscreet record. I had worried over it but, when duplicates were sent after me to Bochum, was relieved to find that there was no entry as to the division. I was rid of that nightmare. At Cambrai one Australian prisoner being asked to name his division declined. The Sergeant Major insisted for a while, then brought an officer, who repeated the question. The Australian, of course, gave the wrong division, when the German promptly retorted, 'You are a liar. I only asked you to see if you would tell me the truth.'

On another occasion one of our prisoners questioned by a German intelligence officer was astonishingly candid. Every question asked was cheerfully answered. The German was delighted to find a man so well informed, yet so unsophisticated. At the close of the interview he was most cordial, smiling and bowing his thanks. Just as he was leaving the room the prisoner called him back.

'I forgot to tell you about the new guns on the Somme,' he said. 'They're a new calibre, very big, but we haven't been able to use them yet.'

'Why is that?'

'Well, to tell you the gospel truth, the shells are so heavy that we haven't enough men to lift them into the gun.'

The German swore volubly and tore up his notes.

On 17 March I was told that a card reporting me wounded and a prisoner in German hands had been sent away twelve days before. It was comforting to feel that my people in Australia knew the worst. On March 10th they had received an urgent cable reporting me wounded and missing, and they had a letter from an officer of my battalion, giving all details available. It was not until May 15th that my people knew officially that I was wounded and a prisoner of war. The German assurance that they had cabled on March 5th was as trustworthy as most things Prussian.

It was from Bochum that I wrote my first letter home and it was, I flattered myself, a masterpiece in dutiful deception. It occupied a page of foolscap and took fourteen days to write. For I was determined that, if possible, no wave of the pen should worry them. That letter was really painted, not written. The concentration in writing four or five words at a time was so great that it left me exhausted.[21]

The first meal in Bochum indicated in one respect at least a better cage. The ration included some good soup, a little boiled meat very well done, potatoes, red cabbage and a little milk pudding. But as time went on the ration shrank and coarsened, my mainstay being a liberal measure of milk from which the cream had been separated. At six in the morning they brought a cup of black coffee without sugar and a thin slice of bread. At nine o'clock breakfast was served, a cup of unsweetened acorn coffee and three small slices of bread, with a small portion of curd-like cheese in which were a few caraway seeds. Like so many things which the Germans genuinely consider a dainty it seemed to me vile, and I was never able to eat it. Another dainty brought on rare or special occasions was a bit of raw fish, not cooked or even smoked, but apparently cut just as the fish was taken from the water. They were greatly puzzled when I declined to eat it.

'But you do not understand; it's so good for you, a delicacy.'

Possibly it was good. I'm quite sure that they consider it so, but I had not been trained to eat raw fish, and they declined to spoil it by cooking. My bit of raw fish was always given to a Russian prisoner. As meals decreased in bulk they increased in aroma. The meat, apparently tinned stuff, was often rotten;

the soup announced itself as soon as the door opened, but I honestly believe that most of the civilians got nothing better. Occasionally meals were forgotten altogether, but that was the fault of the attendants. Another dainty occasionally served, and apparently always eaten raw in Germany, was a very thin rash of bacon. Coming after the fish, my aversion to raw bacon was another matter for wonder.

'It's good for you. What do you want? All you *Engländers* expect roast beef and plum pudding.'

'Not here,' I explained.

On a few occasions they brought me a small piece of smoked fish which had evidently been stored for years and had turned green.

For a long time at Bochum it was a case of next door to death. For three months I was in solitary confinement, with not even a book to break the dreary monotony. Week after week I had very little sleep, all the while suffering almost intolerable pain. No trouble was taken about bed sores, and these were soon added to my other miseries. One of these sores had finally eaten so far into my back that it could no longer be either ignored or endured, so one day they turned me over and poured raw benzene into it. On my emaciated limbs the skin seemed dead and black, and peeled away in flakes. The flesh had almost wasted away. In the third month of captivity my weight, originally 12½ stone, was reduced to about 6½ stone. My face was gaunt and colourless, my hair, never cut or combed, was a curling, matted mass. For weeks they refused to shave me; for three months, in this hospital named St. Elizabeth, they refused even to sponge my body. One doesn't care to dwell upon such unpleasant detail, but this is mainly a chronicle of Hun hospitals and Prussian mercy. My body, of course, was in a filthy state, for ointments and other matter adhered. Care was certainly taken to cleanse a narrow strip just about the wounds, and to prevent infection, but in every other way I was brutally neglected.

For months I received no mails from home. My first Red Cross food parcel came in the sixteenth week of captivity. The constant discharge of pus from the wounds worked even through two squares of black sheet that were placed under me, and soaked into the mattress. There were other English prisoners of war in the hospital, but for a long time none of them were allowed to visit me. It was solitary confinement, with dirt, degradation and pain superadded. My conviction was that they had determined to drive me 'mental' and but for a one little decorative detail of that cell they would probably have succeeded. Near the ceiling the greenish grey wall had its one note of relief in a coloured frieze. Counting the dots of colour in that frieze was my mind's salvation. First I would count them singly, then by twos and threes, hoping that the totals would not agree, so that I might count them all over again. Even counting dots of paint upon a prison wall is poor recreation, but after an hour's thinking I always found myself taking tally again, counting, conjuring. If suffering is part of man's inheritance I got at Bochum all that was coming at me.

With the help of morphia I could generally sleep for an hour, the rest of the night as just staring into darkness, suffering, thinking. With the mind thus void, strange thoughts come into it; some of them perhaps come to stay. That I should have gone mad I have little doubt, but, with the belief once established that it was their will to drive me mental, came the same obstinacy that helped me, I believe, to fight successfully against death at Cambrai. My body at that time seemed already doomed to living death. I could move only my arms. Even the smallest trifles became important. At midnight the German sentry, who stood guard outside my prison, was relieved. He would go to the next room, and it was a relief even to hear him throw his boots upon the floor.

What wattle walks I took in imagination then! It was autumn in Australia, but that mattered not. Memory may supply abroad even that which Nature denies at home. In the good land beyond the sea, peopled with happy memories, it was always spring time.

Twice a day my wounds were dressed by a Russian Pole who, having been in German hospitals for fifteen years, was in sympathy wholly German. Even with such experience in a land which claims superiority in surgical science as in so many other things, his knowledge of cleanliness as a detail of hospital treatment seemed to be wholly elementary. And there was no excuse for it. Soap might be scarce, but water was abundant. Once a week they moved me, and then for twenty-four hours came fresh agony before I could settle comfortably down again. It was at the close of one of those regular pain swells that they brought me an air-cushion to ease the pressure of the bed sores. I knew that if I moved the pain would begin again, so refused it. A couple of days later I asked for it, but the attendant said, 'No, when everything is offered again, you'll learn to take it. Now you may grin and bear it.'

After forty-eight hours he evidently thought I had been punished enough, so brought back the cushion. He was in some ways a queer contradiction, solicitous, careful in the treatment of wounds, indifferent as to anything else. He would wash carefully around about the wounds with methylated spirit, further clean them with peroxide of hydrogen, but, though I implored him to do it, he never once sponged my body, a great concession being a small bowl of water for the face. He differed wholly with the surgeon as to the possibilities of my case, and I was surprised to find the German doctors frequently listening to him attentively, even adopting his suggestions. After about two months I got my first shave. Two boys brought in a huge can from which they lathered my face, and I was happily unaware then that the same pot had just done the round of the wounded Russian prisoners. The Russian is, by choice and habit, dirty; he is also frequently diseased. 'Where ignorance is bliss 'tis folly to be wise.'

One day, to my astonishment, the door of my cell-ward was opened and with a, '*Ha! Engländer!*' and two German

NCOs walked in. After a few remarks of a rather silly nature, one of them opened a newspaper and showed me a picture of the famous L Battery at Néry. All the guns excepting one were knocked out and the only surviving gunner was firing that one at point blank range.

'*England kaput. Deutschland über Alles!*' one of them remarked. '*Gott strafe England!*'

'*Ja, ja!*' I grinned. '*Gott strafe England und England strafe Deutschland!*'

One of them took it very nastily indeed, the other who had some sense of humour laughed loudly at his friend's annoyance. About an hour later the angry one returned with a paper upon which some questions were written in French. The first was:

'You call us barbarians and say that you are fighting the cause of Civilization. Why then do you use black troops to fight against civilised white men?'

'They are not fighting civilised peoples,' I wrote in reply. 'They are fighting Germans. No people guilty of such atrocities as you committed in Belgium and France could call themselves civilised, and no black man, even if he were an ignorant savage, could possibly do worse.'

Again he stamped about in a rage, yelling, 'It's not true!' He had a big voice but a rather weak intellect, and with another '*Gott strafe England!*' he finally disappeared.

My experience of the Hun in all his forms, *kultured* and otherwise, may have been unusually unfortunate, but it seemed to me that while his devotion to his Kaiser and country was undoubted, the deficiency both in his mental equipment and moral standpoint is that 'sporting instinct' and sense of fair play which so conspicuously animates the Briton. It is especially lacking in the Prussian, who could in no circumstances be a sportsman. His code is better suited to crime than chivalry.

A queer experience commenced when I had only been a few days at Bochum. One day I noticed the door open very slowly, then it was pushed a little farther, so slowly that I had lots of time to imagine some new injury or insult from a bright particular NCO, who visited me frequently but never apparently with any other purpose than to bait and abuse. When the door had opened, a foot, a face slowly filled the space. And such a face—old, rugged, with a cavernous mouth wide open and only a few black stumps of teeth left at intervals. Then the face slowly distorted into a grin, until one felt uneasy. It seemed as if the whole top of the head were lifting like a lid from a tea pot, for the apparition was a German woman. Day after day she came thus to stare silently for a long time, then disappear, fading out like the grin of the Cheshire Cat of Alice in Wonderland. It went on for weeks, and in my mental condition had a most depressing effect.

Chapter 14

Prisons and prisoners

Came the day when the first strength exercise was undertaken. It was coupled with the happy news that I would soon be transferred from Bochum, where all the room was required for German wounded. There was no longer, as at Cambrai, the high hope that any change must be for the better. To know the Hun is to lose hope. The first experiment was in being lifted to the edge of the bed—and falling helplessly back again in a faint. Next day the aides held me for a little while, but the test ended with another faint. It was a case of forcing one to strength that might have been reached by easier stages, so they carried on. With support I was soon able to sit for three minutes in a chair, without becoming unconscious. Though months of neglect and ill-treatment are not to be remedied by a few days' attention, I was able with resolution to sit up for half an hour on the fourth day. The gaping wound in the side, though bandaged, was still open, and it was months before it closed. About a week after the commencement of these exercises, I was put in a wheel-chair and taken along the corridor to where sunlight came through a big window. It was the sunlight of heaven, such divine relief to the gloom and solitude of a cell, and in June the weather was becoming pleasantly warm. This went on for a few days, when I was placed upon crutches, and, with the Belgian friend steadying me from behind, entered on another acrobatic phase.

Life was less gloomy. I could see across the courtyard and, though the outlook was chiefly bare walls, it was something to have the walls. In the chapel attic opposite were some Belgian prisoners. One whistled to attract my attention, and then, gripping the bar with one hand, as I happened to be doing at the moment, started to scratch himself in imitation of a monkey in the zoo; a bit of a pantomime that was irresistibly funny. 'Iron bars' in this case quite clearly suggested 'a cage'.

At first, and even with the help of 'Belge', I could only hobble for about a chain on crutches, and once when my pal left me for a few minutes I came a terrible cropper and had to be carried back to bed. The wound bled badly for some time, the blood being quite black. My broken right leg also turned quite black from the toe up to the thigh fracture.

One day hobbling about the hospital square I was attracted by the strange conduct of a Belgian prisoner. He would follow me, staring and silent. When I stopped he would halt, still staring. 'Do you wish to speak to me?' I asked, and offered him a cigarette. He at once fell upon his knees and commenced to pray. When I tried to get him up, he burst into tears. He was one of many 'mentals' manufactured by German 'discipline', and the great difficulty was to get him to eat anything. Once I met him carrying an open tin of sardines, and, as he seemed to follow me always, his mates suggested that I might take him into the ward and persuade him to eat. After taking a mouthful myself I would offer him some, but he just picked it up, stared and put it down again. A few days later, however, they managed to induce him to both talk and eat.

Although a Belgian he had lived in England before the war and joined the King's Own Manchester Regiment. He had been taken prisoner in the early fighting on the Somme, and some of those who knew the poor chap's story said that he had been driven 'mental' by German cruelty. They do take the keenest delight in inflicting even mental torture. Before I commenced to receive parcels from the Red Cross, both German doctors and non-coms never missed a chance to jibe about my country having no use for me.

'Why don't they send you food?'

When it did come, they searched every packet, rigorously probing even into the meat tins to see if anything were concealed there.[22] The one thing that perpetually puzzled them was that nothing in our food parcels was 'substitute'. It did more than anything else to convince the intelligent that the stories told in their propaganda papers about England's starvations were 'hot air'.

On that floor was an Alsatian, who had been sentenced to ten years' imprisonment for refusing to fight against the French. When it might be done safely he spoke his feelings freely. There were many such cases as his where men of French parentage refused to fight their countrymen. He and his brother had been sent to Turkey, where his brother was killed and he was three times wounded. He had also fought against British troops in the North and, after being once wounded, refused to go out into the trenches again. He, with seven other Alsatians who had been sentenced to four years' imprisonment, was kept in one small cell. When the war was over and he completed his sentence he would, he said, go to England or France. There was no doubt at all as to where his sympathies lay. He just hated the Bosche. The Germanising of Alsace had evidently been an imperfect job.

All this time we had little news of war, save when it concerned success for the Central Powers, but 'the blonde beast' himself was an unfailing war barometer. When he was more brutal, more intolerable than usual, the Germans were winning; when he commenced to fawn a bit, to repeat the formula 'We are not such bad fellows as they say', something unpleasant had happened to them. The prisoners of different nationalities were not kept apart at Bochum, and sometimes the mixing had a sinister aspect. Many of the boys were convinced that Russians who reeked of dirt and disease were put into their compound with the sole object of infecting them, and it leaked out that this was done by direct order from German headquarters and was particularly desired in the case of the French. They wished, perhaps, to make them better acquainted with their Allies, for in all sorts of devilry the Bosche is highly efficient.[23]

Under the convention the Germans should have paid me a weekly allowance, but for months I never received a mark, the first payment was not until I reached Karlsruhe. From the few marks which the boys left I was permitted to buy a small bottle of beer each day as a substitute for acorn coffee. The price at first was about 2½d., and it was not even 'Neer Beer.' Of the two hops originally used, one must have hopped out before they corked it. The cost immediately began to hop too, first to 5d., then to 7d. a bottle. Their own supplies were so poor that they wished to discourage me from buying any.

One day, when I was hobbling down the hospital corridor, the Hun sentry took off his cap and put it on my head. I sent the thing flying, carefully brushed my head, and threatened him with one of my crutches. His object was to raise a laugh at my expense amongst some civilians who were then in the hospital. Later I complained to one of their non-coms, who said he was only having a joke.

'If a British soldier played that sort of a joke with a German, he would get cells for it. It's an indignity, and if it happens again I'll report it to the officer in charge of the district.'

Whenever I passed that sentry again he jumped to the salute instantly.

Although many prisoners in working compounds about Bochum tried to escape, I heard of none who got through, and the penalty of failure was 'heavy punishment' with a German inflection. They kept trained dogs, a type of wolfhound, to track the fugitives by scent. When a prisoner escaped the dogs were immediately taken to his bed or given some of his left clothing to smell, so that they might get the scent, and the fugitives hit upon rather an ingenious plan of baulking them. They would save pepper from their Red Cross parcels and, before leaving, dust it freely over their bed and clothing. One sniff was sufficient for the hounds; they lost all interest in the runaway. Of course the Huns discovered the trick and no more pepper came in Red Cross parcels, while most of the drugs were also 'commandeered,' for what reason was not explained.

On one occasion an angry prisoner drew his clasp knife to a sentry and thenceforward the points of all knives were broken off. Most of the sentries were home service men who, unfit for active service, had never been to the front, but that only seemed to make them the more brutal. It was very noticeable indeed that the few guards who had fought in the war were invariably more humane and considerate. That was my own and I think almost every prisoner's experience. The home-staying Hun was all *Kultur*. The searching fires of war, had, in the others, discovered some humanity.

However strict the discipline of the Bosche may have originally been, prisoners who had money, all furnished in the form of special camp notes, had no difficulty in bribing sentries to arrange with civilians for a supply of clothes, a compass, map and other outfit for an attempt at escape. Their 'poverty, if not their will' consented. Of course the prisoners picked their men and tested them freely in little and innocent purchases before asking for things the purpose of which could not be concealed. The sentry who had compromised himself in little things was then afraid to report them. Money meant much to them, because prisoners told me that they frequently saw German soldiers pick up old jam or milk tins from Red Cross packets which had been thrown away, and scrape them out, mouldy bread or biscuits being also gathered. Any prisoner who possessed a couple of cakes of soap found bribery easy, and there were few, if any, instances of prisoner being 'given away'. There was never a case of the recaptured prisoner 'giving away' a sentry, however brutally they treated him.[24]

The irony of Fate was especially illustrated in the case of three fellows who tried to escape from Bochum. They got well away, reached and actually crossed the borders of Holland without knowing it. At that point the boundary jutted out in a cape or salient. The poor fellows went out of sanctuary on the other side and walked right in to the arms of the German sentries.

Another trick of the enemy proved effective until prisoners got to know it. About three miles from the frontier there was a line of posts with notices printed in Dutch, the purpose of the ruse being obvious. Many were taken in by it when just upon the edge of freedom. Later they were careful not to reveal themselves until they were many miles beyond the frontier. The hope of escape, whatever the risks or the punishment, was general. Few were content to sit still and see it out. They were rarely docile and made no secret of their feelings. Men, who in ordinary life would have had every regard for the contentions, had none for German feelings. The road to the cemetery passed close to Bochum hospital, and there were many civilian funerals. Few passed without some for the prisoners cheering and calling out, 'Hooray, another dead Hun!' and before the Pacifist can justly criticise their conduct he needs just a little of their experience.

The Russian Pole who had for a time bandaged and cleaned my wound was about that time given an extra job of white-washing, and had little time to spare for patients. He left me without any attention for sometimes five days at a stretch, and by that time the stench of escaping pus was so intolerable that no one else would take on his neglected duty. This continued until within about a fortnight of my transfer to Karlsruhe, when I was again bandaged daily.

Of all the prisoners held in German compounds the Russian was the most hopeless. Their surrender was complete, their servility abject, the only excuse being that for them came no food from abroad, no comforts of any kind. I watched them often, dull, heavy-featured, dirty and diseased, driving carts through the streets, doing all sorts of work without a guard, with neither hope nor thought of escape, underfed, badly treated, yet always docile slaves. The German understood them as thoroughly as he despised them. They had little or nothing to eat. Other prisoners, getting food supplies, passed on their thin soup to the Russians who drank it by gallons until they became bloated and dropsical. It seemed to me that 80 per cent of them had dropsy, their flesh being in such a state that if you pressed it with your finger the impression remained. It was awful to see them in the food line, always craving for more, yet incapable of protest or resentment, literally 'dumb, driven cattle'. Reformers who talk lightly of Russia's liberty should have seen that sorry sight to realise the utter hopelessness of reformation for Russia ever coming from within. It is one of our great after-war problems, part of the White Man's burden:—

Take up the White Man's burden—
The savage wars of Peace.
Fill full the mouth of Famine
And bid the Sickness cease.
And when your goal is nearest,
The end for others sought,
Watch Sloth and heathen Folly
Bring all your hope to nought

The Russian, as we knew him at Bochum, seemed indeed a hopeless case, without resolution, without self-respect. They would follow anyone who smoked a cigarette until the butt was thrown away, then seize and smoke it to bed rock. Once I gave three cigars to a Russian who absolutely danced with glee—about the one sign of emotion or animation I ever noticed. They seemed to be peasant people and one could see little hope of shaking them into any political impulse that was not purely primitive.

A German non-com who, like most of them, spoke English perfectly, once said to me, 'What do you think of them? They are just about as much use to you as the Austrians are to us. They just about balance each other.'

Out of the experience of Bochum I learned one thing, and that was to set a more just value upon the character and calibre of the Belgian. The Australians in France had 'no time for him', a prejudice mainly due to spy stories. Taking them man for man, I found no finer type, none keener to fight the Hun to the very last extremity. Whatever designs Germany may have had of capturing Belgium either by force or by peaceful penetration is gone for a century at least. In future there should be no footing, no safety for the Hun inside Belgium.

Australian prisoners captured during the Battle of Fromelles on 20 July 1916 are marched towards the rear under the guard of German soldiers. AWM A01552

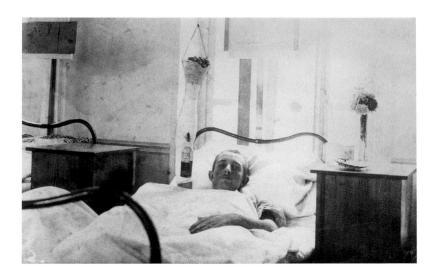

Private Joseph Marrinon, 31st Battalion, at the German field hospital at Douai following his capture at Fromelles on the night of 19/20 July 1916. Wounded Australian prisoners of war were given adequate medical attention in field hospitals behind the German lines, although conditions and treatment often depended on the limited supplies German hospital staff could afford to treat enemy casualties. The economic situation in Germany was already apparent behind the German lines in early 1917, with many wounded Australian prisoners later reporting that their wounds had been dressed with paper bandages. AWM P01114.002

The British officers camp at Karlsruhe, Germany, where Cull was imprisoned after his ordeal at St Elizabeth's hospital at Bochum. Karlsruhe was merely a staging camp where many British prisoners of war were temporarily held before being moved on to other camps. Cull found the wooden barracks and small courtyard simply depressing. AWM P01981.001

Morning appell (parade) at Karlsruhe in 1918. The number of slings, walking sticks and crutches in this photo implies that Cull was not the only wounded officer held here. The barracks may have been depressing, but Cull's experience at Karlsruhe suggests that the camp had the facilities and staff to accommodate the needs of wounded prisoners of war much better than the other camps. AWM H13582

Workers of the Australian Red Cross Prisoner of War Department in London pack food parcels for Australian prisoners held in Germany and Turkey. With regular supplies of food parcels from London, Australian prisoners managed to survive without the meagre German ration. Conditions were so bad at Karlsruhe that Cull was offered thirty pfennigs a day if he gave away the camp ration. AWM H11793

Hannover, c. 1917. Before a prisoner of war could take receipt of his Red Cross food parcel, it first had to be searched by German orderlies for contraband that could be used for the purposes of escape. AWM H13925

The officers camp at Heidelberg, where Cull was briefly imprisoned before his exchange to Switzerland in December 1917. AWM A01702

Australian officers at Krefeld in May 1917, where men who had been captured without serious injury were imprisoned. Most of the men shown were captured at Fromelles on 20 July 1916 or at Bullecourt on 11 April 1917. AWM P08451.002

Chapter 15

A glad goodbye

In every human bulk there are good and bad, and it seemed to be my luck at Bochum to find the German generally at his worst. There was one under-officer in particular whose animosity was endless. Not content with a personal persecution he sought to prejudice others, and generally succeeded. On one occasion, having a couple of marks, I went to the canteen and tried to buy some cigarettes. The non-com in charge, with every indication of active hate, refused to serve me. I laughed and remarked, 'They are not good enough perhaps—"substitute"—like your battalion.'

The word 'substitute' was anathema, a match to the gunpowder of his fury, and there was no hitch in the explosion.

But the under-officer was an unredeemed tyrant. He came to my room often and brought others with him for no other purposes than to indulge his mania for annoyance.

'Look at him, the Australian convict? Is he black?'

The inevitable grin which was my response to every insult seemed to exasperate him the more. His hate followed me from Bochum. One day he came to the ward and said, 'Get up and put on your uniform. You are going away in an hour.'

'Goodo!' I exclaimed. 'But I have no uniform. You people took it away at Bapaume.'

Later he brought me an old field-grey uniform coat, a pair of corduroy breeches and a blue flying corps' cap, for the use of which he said I must pay eighteen marks a month.

I pointed out that I had no boots, and after some foraging he got a pair of old boots which must have spent at least six months on the dust heap. They were hopelessly hard and wrinkled, with the toes turned up. I tried to get them on, but it was quite hopeless, and after another burst of swearing he soaked the boots in a bucket of water for an hour and beat them into shape, or out of shape, with a stick until I managed with difficulty to draw them on.

An hour later he returned with my guard for the journey, as fully a little caricature of the conquering Prussian as I ever encountered. He was about forty-five, and some five feet in height. He came in as advance guard to an enormous sabre, the greater length of which rattled on the ground behind him. Never a Kaiser rattles the sword more frequently or flamboyantly than this manikin. Next he produced an automatic revolver and started to load it.

'This is for you,' he said, 'if you attempt any tricks.'

I nodded acknowledgements and smiles, appreciation of his dramatic powers, but the thought of a poor crippled casualty attacking even this emblem of German authority was too funny. The tyrant appeared with the usual explanation, 'This is the Australian convict.'

It was his last chance and he made the most of it. Taking away my crutches he handed me a stick. A few days previously I had received underclothing in my Red Cross parcel, and he started to hang this kit around my neck with the remark, 'If you swine-hounds get these things you must carry them.'

The Pole, who was present, protested and threatened to report to the medical officer, so the kit was dropped on the floor and left there. I was compelled to walk to the station as well as I could, dragging the maimed leg after me, and every second of that journey was sheer torture. I had to grind my teeth hard to hide it. I left Bochum in a bombardment of sneers.

'Goodbye, you swine-hound. You are going where you will get a taste of the bombs that your airmen drop on us.'

The Pole told me just before leaving that he had heard the under-officer tell my military Tomb Thumb to give me a bad time on the war. 'Barkis', or what there was of him, 'was willing.' Originally I was rather under the average height, but one curious effect of never being on my feet for months was that I had grown 3¼ inches, and quite towered over the guard, who was making the very most of himself. The contrast seemed to cause amusement. I noticed on the way to the station many people pointing at us and laughing, because whenever the little one gave an order he roared it in the best German military manner. There was first a short tram ride, and after I had been bundled into the tram the Little Corporal would not permit me to sit down, thought there were many vacant seats. Unable to stand for any length of time, I fell exhausted against the back of the tram. The hate of the bully of Bochum still followed me. While waiting at the railway station I was permitted to sit, even graciously allowed to smoke. My mixed uniform gave the civilians about the impression that I was either Belgian or French, and they were most tolerant until the Corporal remarked: '*Australisch—Engländer!*'

Then their stares and jests turned to jeers. The hate was not yet exhausted. Finally I was taken into the train and ordered to stand in a corner while the Little Corporal prepared for the worst by drawing his sabre, placing it on the seat ready to hand, and sitting down with his revolver ready between his knees. It was all most imposing—and in a manner flattering.

At the utmost I could only stand for about three minutes and things soon began to swim. I was falling in a faint, gripping the window frame desperately, while the Little Corporal watched and smiled. I would have been down and out but for a young lady sitting opposite, who sprang from her seat, dragged me over and made me sit down while Frederick the Great scowled. In spite of his sour glances she was exceedingly gentle and kind, and I was much touched when she handed a little child who was with her some chocolate, telling her to give it to me. On recovering I stood up to allow the lady to take her seat again, but she motioned me back and took a seat opposite.

After Bochum a little kindness like that sank deep in one's heart. I had believed my hatred of the whole German race to be so great that nothing could ever again lessen it, but at the first touch of kindness it all melted away, and that German woman was an angel. She spoke of the beauties of the Rhine and sorrowfully the woes of war, was so much the true woman that from my heart welled up a fervent, 'God bless you!' Frequently she pointed out places of antiquity or of interest along the Rhine, until the Little Corporal became obviously uneasy. Here was a countrywoman most kind to one of the hated race, treating him actually as if he was a human being! His conscience seemed to prick him. He was disobeying orders from Bochum, so at Coblenz he solved the difficulty by removing me to another compartment.

Wherever I had to walk, he hurried and hustled me. At one station I was within six feet of a water tap, but he refused to allow me to take a drink. He had food on the journey, I had none. Being unable to carry it, I had left my food parcels behind, and the meal at 11 am before leaving Bochum was the last for that day. At one place the Corporal relaxed sufficiently to point with an air of majesty to a colossal monument, built to celebrate their victories in 1870. The great bluff upon which it towers is the eastern wall of the Rhine. From the monument I understand one can look over the French country as far as the Vosges, where the first battles of 1870 were fought.

At one change of trains I was taken by mistake into a first-class compartment, and a couple of German officers who sat opposite immediately objected and told the Corporal to remove me. When he explained that I was a Captain their tone completely changed, and one of them told the Corporal to find a seat for me. Later he came over and started a conversation, explaining that he had been in business in Manchester for about eighteen years.

'What do you think of the war?' he asked.

'Oh, it's quite all right.'

'Not by any means right for you. How long do you think it will last?'

'That will depend entirely on you people.'

'How—in what way?'

'Well, it's just a question of when you will be prepared to accept our terms.'

'Oh, rot,' he retorted. 'Look at our military and economic position!'

'We are gaining strength, you are losing it,' I said. 'And your economic position won't bear investigation at all.'

He fell back for a while upon the old theme of ruined London and starved England.

'You have been in England. You don't believe that.'

'Well time will show.'

'Yes, about two years,' then dropping my voice to an undertone so that the other should not hear, I said, 'You are a German officer, and you are bound in decency and for the sake of your service to say that sort of thing. If I were in your position, I should do exactly the same thing myself. One has to play the game.'

He looked at me hard, gave a bit of a nod, and was silent for a long time.

'My belief,' he said, 'is that victory will come to none of us in this war. It will be fought to exhaustion—and stalemate.'

Amongst the most enlightened Germans that, I am convinced, was the general belief, the best hope. Before returning to his seat the officer said something in German to my guard, and this time I felt sure it was not a repetition of the Bochum orders.

Chapter 16

The Rhineland

The fact of being Germany's unwilling guest, a cripple and a sufferer to boot, did not prevent me from enjoying, in between certain episodes of humiliation, that delectable journey by the historic Rhine. At Bochum there was nothing beautiful. The grimy hand of industry has soiled all the countryside, but with its black smoke and hundreds of chimney stacks left behind, my face was ever pressed close to the carriage window. The first part of it was through the picturesque district of the Ruhr, which unites with its natural fertility other wealth in coal and ores. The only saddening thought was that so many of our boys were at forced labour there for a wage of threepence a day and a ration of war soup. A few miles further on we sighted Essen, the greatest asset of Prussian militarism, the pride of Germany in Peace or War. Perched upon an eminence Krupp's great works of war seemed very peaceful and picturesque on this spring day. Two flags floated over one massive tower and these were pointed with pride by the Corporal as a sign that the 'Great Kaiser', one of the chief shareholders as well as overlord, was then on a visit. The alluring thought occurred, 'Isn't it possible to bomb these works and get perhaps two birds with the one stone?'

It was on reaching the Rhine, which we crossed at, I think, Duisburg, that the romance of the journey began. For a poet there may have been 'peasant girls with deep blue eyes and hands that offer early flowers' but nothing of that sort of a prisoner of war. Yet the great river was a fine sight, and buzzing with activities, little steamers perpetually passing up and down with trails of barges. But there were apparently no passenger boats. The rail runs with the river and all travel is by train. It gives one a rare outlook. After Duisburg the Rhine is left for a time, and we passed through one of Germany's great manufacturing areas, from which her industrial wealth in silks and cottons were spread wide over the earth, but at Dusseldorf was again that ever charming alternation of meadow, wood and field. With a glance at Neuss, at one time belonging to the Hanseatic League of towns, we rush on to Cologne, having followed up the river for about three hours.

'Is it not beautiful?' asked my lady benefactress, and I agreed that it must be the most beautiful part of Germany.

For miles there were nothing but cherry gardens between the line and the stream. On both banks the cliffs often rose a bit back from the river, and between cliff and water were nestling villages, old churches and country houses. Then one passed to the castles area, where almost every crag seemed to be crowned with the ruined keeps of feudal times. No castle was ever built away from a cliff; everything was weathered grey with age. The wonder was how they built upon such inaccessible foundations; the reason for it was obvious enough. Germany had robbers then as now, romantic, possibly not less brutal. The cultivation was all in little fields like those of England, fields without fences or hedges but, as in Southern France, with occasional lines of poplars. In cultivation there was severe economy, every slope and hill being terraced for vines, everywhere turnip fields, yet nowhere any sign of livestock. The field workers were nearly always women, again as in France old men and old women, scarcely ever a young man. If war had robbed the pleasant lands of France of their youth and vigour, it had also called away youth and strength from the valley of the Rhine. Germany, although unravaged, was not unscathed.

At railway stations they stood around and stared, but at one place, finding that I was the detested *Engländer*, crowded around and spat at me until the officer mentioned drove them away. On another station was a company of soldiers at ease. One of them who spoke French called out, as one soldier to another, 'How are you?' We met many troop trains, all moving one way—down the Rhine, all bound for that Western Front which was eating up men by millions. Wherever soldiers drilled, they were usually very young—conscription classes called up before their time. But how very quiet and peaceful all the villages seemed! Later on quite a number of civilians, business men who looked like commercials entered the train. They talked little of war; their conversation was all of mines, shares and stocks, mostly Westphalian, the huge profits that were being made, the big dividends paid out of the blood and ruin of Europe. I thought then that the Rhine valley was the most beautiful land I had ever beheld, and having seen Switzerland, think so still. There is this difference between them—Switzerland is grand, but the Rhine is beautiful.

Cologne is a fine city, well laid out, and as we reached it, its bells clanging and soldiers marching suggested a *liaison* with the Western battle front, and I wondered whether we had a set-back. I could not help wondering how Cologne would have felt after such a bombing raid as the Germans had given many of our unfortified places.[25]

After a dull stretch to Bonn, one reached Rhine beauty again as we approached Coblenz, where for about thirty miles the train runs right by the water's edge and kaleidoscopic changes bring constant wonderment. It is the land of enchantment, full of picturesque little villages that are unforgettable. It was always a feeling of satisfaction that, whatever happened next, whatever lay ahead, I had seen the last of my Lady Bountiful, whose kindness had done more than she knew to soften a foreigner's hatred of all things German.

Nowhere along the Rhine, as far as I knew it, was there any place so strong strategically and yet more pleasant to look upon, than the great fortified city of Coblenz. On the east the Westerwald and Taunus, on the west the Hunsrück and Eifel mountains jut up as great natural ramparts of rugged beauty. The junction of the two great rivers, the Rhine and the Moselle, give it immense importance which the Hun strategist has not overlooked. One recalled the historical fact, and at the same time something of the grey antiquity of the town, that, before the time of Christ, fortifications were built here, not to protect, but to oppose German liberties. Here, after all the ages, Germany was still building its castles of unjust ambitions to become pawns of sacrifice in the moves of a lost game.

As we approached Karlsruhe, even my 'Fredrick the Great' seemed to realise that he was the nearer to humanity in being further from Prussia. Instead of hustling and scowling, he all at once became considerate.

'Go easy—no hurry!'

He, who had refused to let me drink at a wayside tap, even brought me a cup of water with his own fair hand. It was all a matter of geography; the further south, the less savagery.

'I am taking you to a hotel,' he explained, and I looked forward gratefully to something of the comfort that was given to officers of his own country at Donington Hall. 'But you must walk,' he said, and that was the painful end to a picturesque journey.

Almost fainting from pain and exhaustion, I dragged myself somehow to the hotel. Sentries challenged and then passed us. The outside view of the hotel had realised every expectation. Inside I was formally handed over and the Corporal got his receipt. The 'swine-hound' was delivered. I was taken in a lift to the third floor and handed over to a sentry who led me along a bare corridor, opened a door, switched on the light, motioned me in, and with one remark, 'Lights will soon be out', locked the door. For a moment I could only stare in blank amazement, and then in spite of the fact that I was very tired and very hungry, I burst into laughter. A hotel—the incongruity of it! Two iron cots stood close together, the thin palliasse on each sparingly stuffed with wood shavings. Each cot had two cotton blankets, a dirty cloth in lieu of a sheet. This was my apartment. It promised little, realised much that was not unexpected. In the dark the blood-suckers began their work. It was a nest of vermin.

Life in the trenches accustoms one to many things that in peace time are revolting, but this was a Karlsruhe hotel. There is no more generosity in German vermin than in German men; terms in which the difference is not always noticeable. Their tactics were those of Hindenburg—attack in masses. Daylight came slowly after a sleepless night, and I made further examination of my cell. It was about 10 feet by 7 feet, and the frosted window, through which a dim light came, was duplicated and strongly barred. A few inches separated the two windows so that if one scratched a patch in the first he would still be unable to see anything but glazed window beyond. On the table some other unfortunate had scratched a menu:—'Breakfast, coffee; lunch, soup, potatoes or sauerkraut; tea, do., do.; Twenty-four hours' ration of bread issued each morning.'

This cell had been specially fitted for two occupants, the idea being that they were certain to talk, and that the quiet listener outside the door might hear something to his advantage. I learned afterwards that officers had been kept in this vermin-infested cell for weeks. It was enough to drive one mad. A Russian brought some coffee for my breakfast, the sentry standing by to see that he kept his mouth shut. When I spoke to him he was immediately hustled into the passage. Next time he put his finger across his lips as a warning for silence.

I was in no very pleasant mood when a non-com appeared with more papers to be filled in.

'What is your regiment?' he asked.

'We have no regiments,' I answered.

He brought an officer who spoke English. I explained that our organisation was different to that of the British, that I was an Australian, and that we had no regiments. He cursed me freely for a fool, and asked,

'Where is your AIF badge?' He knew the sign.

A little later, upon my asking when my wounds would be dressed, he seemed much surprised, and said, 'What—have you an open wound?' and on seeing it he said, in genuine concern, 'Oh, this is terrible. I must bring the doctor to you at once.'

'If you get bandages I can do it myself.'

'Oh, no,' he protested, 'I couldn't possibly take the responsibility—the doctor must see you.'

The doctor, an old fellow of about sixty-five, was much surprised on learning that I had taken a long train journey in such a state.

'I will have you bandaged and taken away at once. This is no place for you, and you must not attempt to walk.'

'I had to walk last night,' I remarked.

'It was a great shame,' he burst out. 'It was cruelty. We will carry you.'

One of the stretcher-bearers who came was a red headed joker, always jovial. The other had been a student before the war and spoke good French.

'We are not Prussians down here,' he observed. 'You are in Baden and will be well treated. English are well thought of here.'

So on a beautiful sunny day I was carried through the streets of Karlsruhe. Again streets thronged chiefly with old men, women and children, streets kept wonderfully clean and neat in spite of the absence of men—to the infirmary attached to the officers' *Lager*, in which were confined about 300 French and English officers. A contrast struck me at once. At Bochum every civilian, however badly fed, seemed to be well dressed.

Everyone carried a cane. There was always lots of 'swank'. For war time, indeed, their apparel was particularly fine, but I saw them always at their best on Sundays, when they visited the wounded in hospital. Here in Karlsruhe everybody was poorly, even shabbily clad, seemed to be utterly weary, with little interest in anything. Yet so strong was the sense of order that the town continued in apple-pie order. Prosperity was for the coal mining, the industrial districts. Down here was patience and poverty.

Chapter 17

In Karlsruhe *Lager*

M y first impressions of Karlsruhe had been depressing
beyond description. For just a little while it seemed
that I only got release from one kind of German hell to enter
another. The bitter irony of it made me laugh the night before,
but there are two kinds of laughter and one has no mirth in
it. In spite of its wires, the first view of Karlsruhe *Lager* was
interesting. I had been saddened too by the sight of the town.
These old, grey, reposeful buildings seemed to hide much in
silent suffering. One had the feeling that not here was the
cause of war, but only much of its unhappy consequences.
That city which should have been a centre of quiet peace was
full of sorrow, all because militant Prussia in its arrogance had
torn up a scrap of paper that held nothing more valuable than

its pledged word, its national honour, the mere consequences of which were death, devastation and untold agonies.

The worst part of Karlsruhe was the wall about seven feet high, which shut off the prisoners from a view of the outside world. On top of the wall was about eighteen inches of barbed wire, and six feet inside the wall a strong barbed wire barrier about six feet high. Prisoners were forbidden to venture between the fences, were warned that if they even touched the inner wires they might be shot, but the rule was never enforced. The sentries posted inside and out were all of the *Landsturm*, for the most part elderly men. They wore the field grey of the German Army, but as headgear a curious kind of box helmet, flat on top and with a little brush in front of it that in some way seemed familiar. I learned later that these were the identical helmets worn by the German infantry in the war of 1870, which had been kept in store all these years waiting for 'The Day', its opportunities in conquest, and—for the world generally and Germany in particular—its tragedy. The rifles that they carried too were apparently the old 'Needle Gun', about as efficient today as the men who used them. So were the old war and new linked up; the Needle Gun, Germany's first triumph in the manufacture of arms, and the French *Mitrailleuse*, foreshadowing the devastating machine gun of the Western Front.

Carried into the compound I could not, to the great wonderment of the stretcher-bearers, suppress my sense of delight. Under the trees were groups of officers, some reading, some yarning, some basking in the sun. Oh, the delight of being in close touch with comrades again, though at Freiburg some few of those comrades were not too cordial. I was of that young, presumptuous, untaught citizen army, they most of the old military cult with the old military contempt for irregulars. Many of them were taken at Mons. They had little tidings of what the new, unauthorised, wholly irregular Soldiers of Empire were doing, or, knowing it, no longer wondered that Germany was lashing out. While the greatest of British military leaders had wholly recast their ideas, these victims of circumstance had, through no fault of their own, learned little and forgotten nothing. If they sought sometimes to make the intruder in military matters feel his inferiority, they were all the same Britons, brave men, and companions in misfortune.

In the camp hospital there were but three patients, and I was put to bed at once. The orderlies were both careful and kind. On seeing my wounds one little dapper chap remarked:

'You'll be sent to England.'

'Do you think so?' I asked eagerly.

'It's a fair proposition, don't you think?' I shrugged my shoulders, doubting.

'Don't fear,' he said. 'You'll soon be repatriated. It's a certainty.'

Up to that moment I had determined to report at Karlsruhe my treatment on the journey down but, with the cheering talk of repatriation, considered it discreet to swallow my resentment and say nothing. I had written something of my feelings in papers left in my kit at Bochum, and began to worry lest these should be found and used against me.

A German interpreter came and explained that he must search me, but soon satisfied himself that all was right.

'You owe us thirty odd marks,' he said.

'What for?'

'For the latter part of your keep at Bochum.'

I laughed, explained that I had no money, had received none since I was taken prisoner, and so could not possibly pay.

'Oh, you must have received it. You should have received it. There must be something wrong. We'll write and see that you get your money.' He explained that in the meantime, if I had funds in London, I could draw a cheque and get it cashed through the American Express Company. I immediately drew a cheque for £10 and in four days received the money.[26]

As soon as I had settled down the other patients fairly bombarded me with questions.

'Where were you taken?' 'Where have you been?' 'How have they treated you?' 'Did you get your parcels?'

I explained that I had only just begun to receive parcels before leaving Bochum.

'Perhaps you are hungry?'

'Yes,' I said. 'I guess some ANZAC wafers and bully beef would suit me very well now.'

'Are you an Australian?' one of them asked eagerly. 'I'm from New South Wales, but I've lived in Melbourne for years.

Any smokes? No? Well, we'll soon get you something to eat and smoke. We'll fix you.'

And they did. Then I in turn began to question. The silence of months found tongue, speech so long repressed bubbled into words. It was such a relief to find myself amongst Britishers again and welcomed in the grand old way. Jibes, scowls and sneers from faces full of hate had so long been my share of man's companionship that any little act of kindness, the one touch of Nature that makes the whole world kin, deeply affected me. I have mentioned such unexpected occurrences in the changing of my bed at Cambrai, the kindness shown by the lady on the way to Karlsruhe. They were Germans and kindness from them in my experience was so unusual that I am the more glad to acknowledge it, for I cannot forget how grateful I was, how much it meant to me. May Heaven bless them with good and true friends should they ever know the need.

My new Australian friend was Lieutenant Arthur McQuiggin of the 14th Battalion, who had been wounded and taken prisoner at Bullecourt.[27] The other two in hospital were infantry officers, one of whom explained the camp rules. I would find the officials, he said, a pretty decent lot, and Commandant a particularly fine chap. That estimate was a just one. He did all that could reasonably have been expected to make the conditions better for prisoners of war, spoke to us as if we were human beings, not in the Bochum manner as beasts. He had permitted a library for the use of prisoners of about three hundred volumes, chiefly German editions of English works, most of them the Tauchnitz editions well known in Germany, the books being, of course, paid for by the prisoners.

An English Colonel brought me a book and asked me how I stood for food, and on telling him that I had none until parcels could be transferred from Bochum, he said, 'Well, we haven't much, but I'll see what I can do for you.' He brought me a tin of condensed milk and part of a tin of meat.

Some time afterwards the Commandant mentioned one day that he had been eleven years in England attached to the German Embassy, and added, 'Those were the happiest years of my life.' I heard later that he had also been in France upon other employment before the war, and being suspected as a spy, got a hint to leave the country. Still that's all in the business. Let him who is without reproach cast the first stone.

There were about a hundred and fifty officers in the *Lager* of whom about a hundred were receiving parcels. From these a deduction was made for an emergency food pool to help others. There was never enough to go round, but it was a delicious topping off for the German ration. The difficulty in hospital was that, while their Red Cross orderlies spoke French, few prisoners could do it. On hearing me speak a few words of French the attendants appointed me ward interpreter, and I managed somehow to carry off the bluff. It seemed to me now that I must have talked for days after entering Karlsruhe camp.

'Cully, you were just irrepressible,' McQuiggan said to me afterwards, and with my experience of the bad black north, the conditions of this ward seemed luxury. The bed was an old iron cot and we slept upon wood shavings, but there was a print pillow-slip, a rough calico sheet, and two blankets enclosed in a print bag cover. Then we got a change once in six weeks, or two changes in that time if the Neutral Committee were expected to visit. We always knew they were coming at least twenty four hours before they arrived, and the camp authorities were advised much earlier. The orderlies got to work brushing up and making everything cleaner and brighter. They would suggest that the English officers who, in that warm sunny weather were accustomed to knock about in flannels and blazers, should put on their uniform for the inspection which, in that it was never a surprise visit, became something of a farce. The Neutral Commissioner, in this case a Dutchman, was in his inspection of the camp always closely attended by the Commandant. He rarely asked a question. He just took a glance here and there and passed on.

'How are your wounds getting on?' 'Have you been long in hospital?' were the only two questions he asked, and always before one could answer he shot away again. The inspection was wholly perfunctory, though personally I had, as may be realised, little cause for complaint. One has heard much of the Neutral Commission during the war. To be candid, it seemed to me and to others with whom I spoke just distressing duplicity, an arrangement to suit the purposes of the Hun alone. The first doctor at Karlsruhe was decent and always amiable, generally offered us a cigarette, but as a physician he seemed to be a bit careless. His successor, as to whose professional skill there could be no doubts at all, was especially bitter against the British.

Some few weeks after I reached Karlsruhe, Captain Frederick Hoad, another Australian, and nephew of the late Major General Sir John Charles Hoad, was brought in.[28] He too had been very badly treated. Part of the muscle of one leg had been shot away, and in hospital he was so neglected that his wounds were fly-blown. The curious thing about it was their assurance that this had probably saved his leg from amputation, a mystery for which only a professional man may offer an explanation. He had been twelve months a prisoner, the greater part of the time with Russians, Romanians, Belgians and French, to none of whom he was able to speak. In all that period he had no food parcels, and altogether was in a bad way. Soon afterwards he was exchanged and sent to Switzerland, chiefly, I understand, through the interest and intervention of Miss Leila Doubleday and some influential American friends.

It was at Karlsruhe that I met a very good friend in Captain Alexander Hall of the Mercantile Marine, whose steamer *Katherine* had been captured and destroyed by the German raider *Möwe* in the North Atlantic. He was a month on the raider before being landed at Kiel and was sent straight down to Karlsruhe. Our friendship soon ripened into the most sincere regard. We found that we had many ideas and aspirations in common, were both concerned and spoke often about our dear ones at home. He was about the same age as my father—to whom, strangely enough, he bore a strong resemblance—and always called me his boy. I must acknowledge with feelings of deepest gratitude the great help and influence of Captain Hall at that time. If I was in pain, and I still suffered greatly, he was a devoted attendant, looking after me as if I were really his own son. With experience of German hospitals and German hate, my mind had become something of a wilderness of confused thought, full of spiteful and morose feelings. I had almost lost faith in humanity, so long I had known only the Hun with his total lack of generosity or fair play. So much I detested him that I was deaf to every appeal from the Sisters of Mercy at Bochum, even when their entreaties became almost a demand. It was the genial influence of Captain Hall, his broadminded humanity and unshaken faith that mainly helped to restore my faith in my kind, to bring my mind back to a healthy normal state again. I met him when I was broken in body, disordered in mind, and much in need of healing, and his words of cheery hope were of inestimable value. It was a delight to meet him again at Heidelberg, later again in Switzerland, and to share his pleasure when he had the good fortune to be repatriated to Scotland and his dear ones there.

At Karlsruhe there was still a severe economy in food, the menu of acorn coffee, black bread, thin soup, potatoes and carrots, running its baleful course. Without the Red Cross parcels it would have meant slow starvation to many prisoners. At Karlsruhe a cat which came about the hospital suddenly disappeared, and questioning Parnell, one of the French attendants, he said, 'Ah well, we ate it.' Noticing my grimace of disgust he asked, 'Why not? It is all the same as rabbit.'

Amongst the prisoners was a Canadian, Lieutenant G. D. Hunter of the Royal Flying Corps, who had been almost starved to death, the thinnest man I ever saw. When brought down a bullet had gone through the fleshy part of the arm, a wound that with decent treatment should have been perfectly cured in about three weeks. After putting on the field dressing the Germans took him back behind their lines and never allowed him to touch the bandage for ten days. When it was finally taken off in Germany the arm was rotting and had to be immediately amputated close to the shoulder. It was another of very many instances in which carelessness seemed to be a deliberate policy, leading only to one consequence. It meant much to a prisoner's luck where he was taken. In a hospital in Southern Germany, either Baden or Bavaria, he had a fighting chance, but anyone with experience may conjecture how many cases of murder and mutilation must be credited to the Prussian who, wherever you meet him, in the line or behind it, is an abomination, a bully in victory, a cur in defeat, and treacherous always. You may deem this all morbid mania, or hysterical prejudice, but if there is one nationality upon earth that I think I know it is the Prussian. For so long I had little else to do than study him.

Chapter 18

The lighter side

In the canteen at Karlsruhe one was still able to buy a bottle of very light Rhenish wine, but food was dear and scarce. A small tin of sardines cost 3/6; for one fortnight about the end of June or the beginning of July, sugar sold at 1½d. a lump. My wounds had careful attention every day and I was the only one in hospital who still got gauze or cotton bandages. All the others were paper—'substitute.' Lint was very scarce and before I left it was almost impossible to get cotton. That great silent power, the British Navy, was doing its work in the North Sea. Little was said or written of it, but the Germans knew it and their hate was in proportion. They knew and felt it in every operation of everyday life, knew that while the seamen of England maintained this grim, strangling grip upon them their own navy—apart from the submarine—was powerless to resent it.

There was one old corporal of the Red Cross in Karlsruhe whom we called 'Dad' and who referred to us in turn as 'his boys'. He always hung about us at meal times and pleaded for anything that was left over. Although engaged in the camps most of the attendants were fed at home. 'Dad' used to bring his lunch in a handkerchief and pack it furtively away. The lunch was always the same—a hunk of black bread, a raw turnip and a pinch of salt over it. He had two sons, one of whom he told me was permanently injured in a bombing raid on Karlsruhe.

The aviators came over one night when there was a circus just outside the town and, seeing the tents, bombed it in a mistake for a military camp, killing or wounding about three hundred people, of whom over a hundred were children. Immediately afterwards the Germans placed a prison camp on the circus site. 'Dad's' second boy was a Sergeant Major on the Western Front, and he had a conviction that this one would be taken prisoner. He asked one of our chaps to write a note for him saying that he had always looked after prisoners properly, and he believed that if he could get such a letter to his son, with instructions to keep it about him always, it would lead to his being treated kindly in turn. We were able to assure him that Britons in no circumstances, except when surrender was a cloak to treachery, ill-treated prisoners. Strangely enough, before leaving Karlsruhe, I heard that this man had been taken prisoner somewhere around Ypres, and 'Dad' was rather pleased about it. 'We know,' he confided to me, 'that the British always treat prisoners well, though the French do not.' He also told me that his brother, long resident in England and a naturalised British subject, had two sons fighting with the English.

One of the attendants, the student who had not completed his course when war broke out, sometimes spoke to me in confidence. 'Our Kaiser is mad,' he explained. 'We know very well that Prussia forced on this war because her object had been conquest, and she was confident about the strength of her armies. We can't hope to win now,' he added. 'England has spoiled all our ambitions and our people are starving. It takes all I can get to keep me alive. Curse the Kaiser!'

On another occasion he offered the opinion that for Bavaria, at any rate, a German victory would be the worst event. 'Defeat would be our future salvation. No more uniforms, no more clicking of heels and saluting for these damned Prussians. I shall stick my fingers on my nose to them.'

He was no mere grumbler either, but a very fine type of fellow, a superior man in many ways, very friendly and very kind. Indeed nothing that he could do for the prisoners was ever a trouble. He had too a sense of decent dignity, for while 'Dad' hung about, as I have explained, at meal time, the student always made a point of getting out of the way. His views were influenced by no thought of favour. 'Freddy', as he was known to us, dropped a hint one day that we should not trust 'Dad' too far, as he had the reputation of carrying tales to headquarters. 'Striker', another attendant, was the red-headed humorist whom nothing seemed to depress.

There was a Bavarian who had been with the Uhlans, and one day I mentioned atrocities. 'Oh yes, that's the way,' he remarked. 'We did have our fun with the girls,' and he seemed to be rather proud of it. He told me that he was married, talked dolefully about his wife and children who were trying to live upon what would have been sufficient food for one. He was always pleading for scraps to take home to them. He showed us a portrait just taken of his wife and family, and it was horrible. They looked like ghouls. They were, without a doubt, starving.

Outside there was often wonder why Germany had not risen in revolt, but I realised there was little hope of that. The spirit of revolt might exist, but there was nobody behind it. Almost all the men who were fit to fight had reached such a stage of exhaustion that they had no alternative but to submit and suffer. 'Forbidden' had come to be a word full of stern meaning: behind the sentiment of 'Fatherland' was an iron discipline. Both in Northern and Southern Germany the law of the survival of the fittest in its crude barbaric form was being enforced. The weak must fall, so that the strong might stand unencumbered by any sentiment which, in the higher civilisation, means chivalry or practical humanity. How often we heard that the aged and infants were dying in great numbers, that the German cupboard was empty. In many ways they were suffering. Cotton was so badly needed for explosives that its use otherwise was almost denied. Much of the clothing was being made from inferior fibre, most of it obtained, I was told, from a tough kind of mettle. Meat was taboo; the sausage remained, but was more than ever a mystery. The famine in fats was so severely felt, no soap, no candles. About the rumour that they were boiling down their own dead the Germans were always resentful, and explained that it was due to a wrong translation of one of their orders. They always burned their dead, who were wired together in bundles of five, and English officers who saw these trainloads of bundled dead stacked in open trucks say it was a horrible sight.

Under all these circumstances the prisoners of Karlsruhe *Lager* were fairly comfortable. There was no lack of musical talent in camp, and they had managed to hire a piano, so that concerts were frequently held, a German official being always present as censor to see that nothing offensive to German sentiment appeared on the program. On the French national day we were permitted to sing our anthem, but were asked not to 'acclaim' because people outside said that prisoners were having too many concessions, enjoying themselves too much, though we saw little sign of any strong civil feeling upon that point. As compared with Northern Germany I noted repeatedly a change in the sentiment. In Prussia they at least made pretence of admiring Frenchmen who, they said, could do nothing less but fight in defence of their country. For a time at any rate a better understanding with the French prisoners was being very sedulously cultivated. In Baden the great majority were better disposed towards the British and rather hated the French. This was due, without much doubt, to the fact that the flying squadrons which crossed the border to bomb their towns were almost nearly always French.

One day the Commandant read out a list of names amongst which mine was included, and said, 'You are to be repatriated soon.' We exchanged warning glances not to make a demonstration then, but when he had left we became almost hysterical in our congratulations. A few days later 'Dad' explained that we were to leave on July 18th, that we would be send to a port in Holland and a British hospital ship would meet us there. July 18th found us in a fever of excitement. Then came the chilling information that there was a hitch and delay. England, they said, was to blame. There was some dispute as to the ports of exchange, but we might get away at the end of the month. One day after another was mentioned for departure, but as time passed we lost all faith in such rumours. About the middle of September hope revived, but the end of it was the intimation that some were to be transferred to another camp. The intention to repatriate had been genuine enough, for we were examined by medical boards and the papers of exchange prepared. Those eligible for repatriation were men who had lost a leg or an eye, if the doctors agreed in such a case that the sight of the other eye was badly affected or failing. Paralysed and tubercular patients were also included.

From June on for some time the weather in Baden was hot, and about that time the doctors said that they wished in my case to try the sun care. I was carried out every day and laid in the sunshine with the wound exposed. Improvement was very soon noticeable, the wound commenced to heal and a film of skin to form over the gap. The sun cure seems to be very widely practised in Germany. It is not wholly for thrift's sake that children are encouraged to walk to school bare-foot, carrying their books with them. Boys and girls not constitutionally strong are taken in summer to the pine woods of the Black Forest, where, almost nude, they spend as much of their time as possible in the open air. The Australian must have lived for a time in the worst weather conditions of Northern Europe to realise himself as he is—a Sun worshipper—to appreciate the extent to which both his constitution and character have been fashioned and favoured by sunlight.

Whenever food parcels were delayed, 'Freddy' would point to our empty tables and remark, 'England finished— no more food.' But he always got back his laugh and the retort, '*Verdient*. Deutschland finished; no food.'

They were apparently not much worst off in that respect than they had been a year before, although living largely from one potato season to another. Agriculture, like everything else in Germany, had been organised for war. Root crops were their mainstay. Here in Baden fields of red beet, carrots, turnips and potatoes spread far and wide. There was little fallow, every patch was being cultivated, not as a private enterprise, but always 'For the Government'. The two great crops were cabbages and potatoes. I had the impression that, by comparison with beans and peas, the diet specialists declared both these foods to be greatly over-valued. If German opinion is to be judged by its practices, they think otherwise.

One of our interpreters at Karlsruhe was an elderly man, a very quiet, decent fellow, who had formerly been a prosperous schoolmaster. He would talk freely about Germany's condition and prospects when there was no chance of his being overheard by anyone in authority. He too was wrathful with the Prussians and especially the Junkers, saying that it would be a good thing for the people if Germany were beaten. One might 'Damn the Kaiser' to his heart's content almost anywhere in Baden, and be sure of finding the echo peculiar in being rather more virulent. Here, too, they were of opinion that the best they could expect from the war was a draw, with all the combatants reduced to the same dead level of exhaustion. One no longer heard the boast proudly made by a Sergeant Major at Bochum: 'Germany can never be beaten by a nation of tea-drinkers.'

In many ways we realised that we were then occupying probably one of the best prison camps in Germany. True, we saw little outside the *Lager*, which was about two hundred yards square, but with a decent Commandant there was little inside it with which the fair-minded might find fault. In no circumstances would I have complained about the rations, for at that time they were unquestionably doing their best. There was very little punishment, mainly because there were no offences. One officer was sent to cells for referring to the Germans as 'Bosche', a term to which they much objected, and which the French used repeatedly for their annoyance. The attitude of the Commandant of a German prison regulates for good or evil the conduct of the whole staff.

Our food parcels from home were satisfactory, so much so that the camp authorities offered to pay us thirty pfennigs a day if we could relinquish our right to the German ration, so that it might be distributed outside. The sentimentalist may say that we were inhuman to refuse. But there was always this hard fact to consider. We were being asked to help Germany over difficulties which her own ambitions and cupidity had created. It was only when they began to suffer that they ceased to be arrogantly patriotic. To help them by foregoing anything that was our right would have been a sort of treason. It was well for the sake of peace in the future that all Germany should realise the suffering of the war which they had created, suffering which will be a black legend along the Rhine through many future generations. The frothing patriot who thinks that he covers the whole case with 'Kill the Kaiser' has neither thought nor fought. They were trying hard to cover up their needs for strategy's sake. For having admitted at Bochum that they were only getting a small allowance of horseflesh twice a week, a two-inch wafer, in fact, one man was sent to cells for six days.

Once a week prisoners at Karlsruhe were allowed to have a bath, a cold shower outside, a hot bath in the infirmary.

There was an effort to prepare a tennis court in the *Lager*, but this could not be managed. The Commandant, however, brought a set of bowls, and they were able to play the game in a rough way upon hard ground. Another social success was a stage fitted up for a Pierrot show, and it was in absolute defiance of prison rules that the Commandant manages to get them seven suits of thin cotton pyjamas as the basis of costumes. We had the help of a skilled artist for the scenes, and much ingenuity was shown in cutting out little trifles from food tins for decoration. With the means available the stage and costume party were a remarkable success. The Adjutant, a bit of a bully, tried to baulk us at first, but a hint from higher up stopped him. Personally my only worry was still no word from home. The first letter overtook me at Freiburg ten months after I had been taken prisoner. I cannot help thinking that for some reason they were purposely kept back. Many letters which reached me in Switzerland, via Germany, had left Australia eight months before.

Two religious services, Catholic and Protestant, were held every Sunday. The young padre, another of the best German type, visited and conversed with us often. A Captain of the Mercantile Marine, who had been educated in Germany and knew the language perfectly, was also permitted to obtain certain specified German papers and read them to us, but on some days when we assumed that the news was not agreeable, no papers came. It was at Karlsruhe that we got first news of the great offensive against the Italians, and for some time afterwards those in Baden believed it to be the finishing stroke of the war. Of the two propaganda papers widely distributed through Germany, one was called the Continental edition of *The Times*, most of the articles in it being written by a notorious renegade. Another was the Continental edition of a French paper. The war news given in German papers seemed generally reliable, they were honest in mentioning failures as well as success. Occasionally we had new prisoners, flying men whose machines had been crippled and compelled to plane down on the wrong side of the line. Thus we got occasional scraps of news of our own operations in Ypres.

Chapter 19

Moving south

The German spiritual point of view, when one heard it, was often interesting. A Sister of Mercy explained to me that God must punish England, not because the Germans wished it, but because the English, French, Belgians and Russians were really heathen peoples who had ceased to pray at all. Germans, on the other hand, prayed often, so God would listen to them.

'Why do you hate us so much?' the doctor asked me one day. 'I cannot understand it.'

'We don't hate the German people, we only despise them.'

'Oh no, you don't. The trouble is that England, through commercial jealousies, is responsible for the war. We were doing too well. You were jealous of our progress.'

'You were certainly doing well,' I answered, 'so well that we cannot understand why you should have been so infernally greedy. You wanted a place in the sun, a very reasonable desire, but you know that you also wanted the earth with it.'

Referring to the French, the Doctor would say, 'Oh, they are like a lot of children. They are still sore about 1870.'

Occasional small excitements in hospital were due to the eccentricities of 'Freddy' who alternated fits of great violence, which always left him with a strong desire to cut 'Dad's' throat, with ordinary fits of drunkenness. One night after lights out we heard 'Freddy' coming in with a tremendous racket, and I suggested that it would be as well to have our crutches ready. 'Freddy', who was very drunk indeed, turned on all the lights, and had a fixed belief that one of us had just been wounded, so must be bandaged and given medicine at once. He was taken away by a comic figure in a long night shirt. As he had the run of the drug chest and seemed to serve out medicines in a very casual way, we had to examine very closely everything that 'Freddy' gave us.

On several occasions our night bombers flew over Karlsruhe, and for a while there was tremendous commotion. The barrage was always very heavy, all lights were out, and the German soldiers and officials, usually made for shelter while the prisoners were wandering up and down the *Lager* on the lookout for souvenirs and falling shrapnel. When we chaffed the Germans about the fear of the raids, they said that we too should go under cover because a bomb might be dropped on the camp. We told them that as long as the bombs kept dropping we would take our chances.

Postcards of the *Lager* had been 'faked' in a rather clever way. There was a large building used for some military purpose just outside the wires, but that never appeared in camp photographs. The camera, carefully controlled and camouflaged, can lie very convincingly. No point of military interest ever appeared in official postcards, which somehow had the knack of so managing perspective as to make an enclosure a couple of hundred yards look at least four times its natural size. I noticed the same thing later at Freiburg, the shameless pretence of the College quadrangle (the prisoners' only exercise ground) in making out that its twenty-five yards of space was a noble and airy square. Whenever a prisoner's photograph was taken to be sent home he was always posed near the Commandant's office, over one side of which climbed a picturesque creeper. It was not much of an effort in wall-gardening, yet it managed to convey the impression that prison life was mostly spent in a romantic bower. Anyhow, our friends were the happier for the belief, and in this the fake photograph was still wholly justified.

Over the door of the military building mentioned was a rough caricature of a lion, representing England, with a German holding the beast by the scruff of the neck and trouncing him with a cudgel. That Englishman should only laugh at it was a perpetual puzzle. They used to remark upon it often, and generally came to the conclusion that all

Englishmen were 'mental'. The last thing I can imagine is a German who would laugh at being satirised, hear himself called a Hun without becoming, as he always did, violently angry. Possibly the name is too near the truth to be admissible, yet seldom was any other name given to him by prisoners of war. The Hun knows that it will stick.

A popular study in camps was that of languages. Groups of English and French officers would get together every day to learn and to teach, but there was no class for German, through of course we were 'picking up' a little of it. We always explained our indifference to the German tongue on the ground that there would be very little use for it in the outside world after the war.

At first our food parcels came regularly and were handed over with only nominal inspection. Then it was complained that the French had hidden letters in some of their parcels and instructions were issued that they must be opened in the presence of officials, an acknowledgement of the contents given to us and the goods sent to store to be obtained when we required them. Then, if tinned food were required, the tins were opened in our presence and searched before being handed over. One of the immediate results was complaints from several prisoners that packets were missing. The Commandant ordered an enquiry, found that the goods were being taken by one of the men in charge of the sheds, and sent him to cells for fourteen days. After that there was very little pilfering. At one time there was a good deal of theft from Red

Cross en route, but the authorities stopped this by placing an armed guard over them. If well supplied, we always kept a reserve in our lockers, and a prisoner with twenty tins in stock was a 'Capitalist'. Many a time we heard officials of all ranks discussing our food supplies. One side used it as an argument in ridicule of their own U-boat blockade.

'They are well supplied, and their food is real—not "substitute".'

'That is no proof,' was another view. 'Even if the civil population were starving, they would still send the best of everything to their officers.'

In this they merely measured our corn with their bushel. Whenever the military officer and the civilian come together in Germany, the civilian is not left long in doubt as to his place. It is always underneath. The officer is eternally rattling his sword and clanking his spurs, making no secret either of his authority or his contempt. The tremendous social gap between the officer and the non-com was continually demonstrated, and gave point to the regulation which required officer prisoners of war to salute the Hun non-coms placed in authority over them. It was intended for humiliation. At Karlsruhe they were not particular upon that point, but I was told that in Holzminden camp there was much trouble about it. The Commandant there was a General of Division which was badly whipped by the British, so he never missed an opportunity for exacting small revenges. Sometimes of a morning there was a list of perhaps sixty officers for cells on account of small and for the most part unintentional offenses. They had been told, as in other places, that if anyone touched the inner wire he was liable to be shot. One day a Russian thoughtlessly put his hand on the wires and the German sentry shot him. There was great indignation over it and the affair was reported to the Neutral Commission, whose verdict was that the sentry had, in view of the regulation, only done his duty. It was admitted, however, that the Russian was not attempting to escape, that if he had offended against the regulations there was ample time to take other steps. In the circumstances a promise was given that the sentry would be punished for his indiscretion. The punishment apparently took the form of a promotion from private to sergeant, and, of course, a transfer to another camp, which happened to be Karlsruhe. He was pointed out to me there, always an overbearing brute, with never a decent word to say. There he was, in the main, innocuous.

Those who had been for some time in Karlsruhe Hospital always bore testimony as to the kindness of the Sisters. Amongst the men, however, was the moral cowardice that I have already mentioned, the tendency to cringe and funk the future whenever a setback suggested the possibility of their ultimate defeat.

'We are not so bad, are we? We cannot give you better food when we had not got it.'

The Commandant was not too well pleased when he received word that we were to be removed from Karlsruhe to make room for Italian prisoners taken in the big Hun offensive.

'Ach, those greasy macaroni eaters,' he would say contemptuously. 'They are as bad as the Russians and the Austrians. They turned us down and they will do the same for you. They are cowardly, you cannot depend on them.'

His preference for the British officer as against the French was certainly not based upon a greater servility, it was largely, I think, a matter of business. They had more money, were better buyers at the prison canteen, in which the Commandant (a Baron, by the bye) was said to have an interest. While fruits were in season we were able to buy in turn cherries, plums, peaches and apples, all excellent, at 1s. 6d. a pound. Because of their value as an antiscorbutic we bought freely.

Towards the end of October the British prisoners were moved out, the Commandant paying for cabs for those in the infirmary but, as an afterthought, deducting the sum from our pay. He send 'Dad' to the station to give us a farewell drink of what they called mint tea, brewed I fancy from the leaves from the lemon scented verbena, a well known garden shrub often used in Europe as a flavouring for tea.

There was a very general belief amongst our prisoners that officers held by the Germans were being massed in camps along the Rhine as a reprisal for bombing raids, while men were for the most part sent to prisons further in the interior. After the heavy bombing of Treves on the Moselle the enemy apparently concluded that, if the Rhine towns were to suffer, captive officers should share the risk, and I don't think there was a man amongst the prisoners who wished to see the raids suspended on his account. If they would have preferred to see the raiders dropping their pills further North in Germany it was for quite other reasons than concern about their own safety, just a desire, which I strongly shared, that the medicine should be given where it was most needed.

Freiburg, not far from the Rhine, was in close contact with the Vosges. Arriving at the station, we found a car waiting for infirmary cases and about twenty armed guards to conduct the hundred prisoners to the camp. On the platform they were counted over and over; occasionally on the way to camp they were halted and again counted. The sentries were very vigilant, seemed to think that English officers might be expected to disappear as mysteriously as 'the Scarlet Pimpernel'. The new camp was very old, the grey masonry buildings of old Freiburg University, one of those ancient seats of learning in Germany which are always interesting. It seemed to be clean, neatly kept, and its occupants were pulling well together. It was a point of honour that everyone should try and help others, whereas at Karlsruhe there were little factions, elements that wouldn't mix. Hearing that we were coming, a Royal Flying Corps man got the mess together and from their own supplies cooked us a good meal. McQuiggin and myself, being infirmary cases, had a nice room 'all on our own' with a big Bavarian student, an overgrown, lumbering, awkward boy, to look after us. He was a very decent fellow, like the rest much surprised at the quantity of food sent to us once the delivery of parcels, always deranged for the time by transfer to another camp, became regular again. We tried to induce him to buy beer for us outside, but he 'had the wind up' very badly about officialdom, said we might buy wine (port at 14 marks a bottle, table wine at 10 marks) but could not possibly have beer. We were allowed to prepare our own food, a bucket of coal being supplied for each room of eighteen prisoners, and used a stove rather resembling one of our street letter-pillars, the fuel being dropped in at the top.

The first trouble at Freiburg was with the Commandant, who was rather a weak man. His first act on appointment was to prohibit the weekly walk, which had been previously a privilege. Those who were willing to give their word were allowed out on parole under nominal guard for long walks to the picturesque walks near the town. The privilege was valued and of course never abused. But that little incident of the careful counting of prisoners on the road from the station was just another illustration of German authority taking its tone from the top man. They were apprehensive and fidgetty because the Commandant was so. The prisoners at once organised resistance to the regulation, and they had taken the measure of their man pretty accurately. The senior officer was sent first to ask that the new rule be abolished. On refusal there was a demonstration in the University square, and two hundred indignant men managed to make a fine protesting row. It was right in the middle of the town, and the old fellow tried vainly for a time to stop the row, but they refused to listen to him and sent along a list of prison laws to be amended.

Once he had given way the prisoners practically ran the camp. The French parole was not taken because the Germans asserted that it had been broken. The proximity of the Vosges had possibly proved too strong a temptation, though the Frenchmen indignantly denied the charge, asserting that German officers in France having broken the solemn pledge commencing 'On my honour I do agree' etc., were refused parole, and that the French were being punished now, not for their own offences, but as an act of retaliation.

The prison adjutant had been for many years in England engaged in a cotton business. He often said that 'Blighty' was his home, and his one desire was to get back to it and pick up, if possible, the threads of his old business as soon as the war was over. He had the very best of reasons for treating us well, and did so, referring to us, in the familiar English way as 'You Birds' and calling us by camp nick-names. With others I was sometimes wheeled a mile or so outside the town, while prisoners who were fit played football. Again there was a picture show once a week in the old dining hall of the University, which had never before entertained so strange a company. Whether pictures of papers, they were alike propaganda. The films dealt mainly with incidents and episodes of the Italian victory, or general war stuff with a good deal of Hindenburg, who was at the time Germany's war idol.

The continental edition of *The Times* had disappeared. Instead we got the *Gazette de Lorraine* and *Gazette des Ardennes* both of course shameless humbugs, compounded and printed in Germany. The news was as absurd as it was malicious, its purpose very definite. The French authorities, it declared, had realised that England was practically in permanent possession of Calais and the country surrounding it, and when the war was over it would be too late to push them out of it. If the Central Powers were defeated France was to get back Alsace and Lorraine, but England's price for the deal was Calais. The only resentment one felt about a thing of this kind was that the Germans should have so very poor an estimate of the intelligence of both English and French officers as to hope that they would deceive them with such a very shallow 'fake'. If their persistent work in war propaganda brought no better results elsewhere, there had been tremendous waste. The German is so very arrogant, so cocksure himself, that he is almost certain to under-rate his enemy. It all led to good fun; Frenchmen offering in exchange for the evacuation of Calais to hand over the 'Folies Bergère', the only place in Paris, they declared, which in their experience the majority of Englishmen seemed really to desire. That sort of thing being quite incomprehensible to the jokeless German mind, they may have imagined at times they were really 'queering the Entente'. Poor France! *Perfidious Albion*!

Chapter 20

The last of Germany

The French and English of Freiburg camp had no monopoly in the secret service news served up by the propaganda press. About once a fortnight the few Australians there were in their turn stung. In a well-considered and far-seeing article it would be pointed out that the Australians were really the only troops amongst the Allies capable of forcing any results, so they were being used ruthlessly for desperate enterprises. There was, we learned, a double purpose in it, first to get results in war that English troops were not capable of achieving, in the second place to so reduce Australia's manpower that she could not, for a long time to come, achieve that aim which was Australia's dream and England's nightmare: Australian independence, throwing off 'the English yoke'. The synonym for 'yoke' is a very popular word in Germany. The writer, dear sympathetic chap, deplored that Australians should be so blind as not to see England's plot. I met at least one Australian who did see it, or partly saw, but he, poor fellow, was, I'm sorry to say, a victim of German not English brutality, and at that particular time 'mental'. A German illustrated paper often shown to us at that time for our enlightenment was *Die Woche*—or it might have been *Die Bosche*, both its sound and its sense were confusing.

The campus of the old university, as I have mentioned, was about a chain in length, though the camera made it a noble space, but its chief fault was that it only got the sunlight for about two hours every day. Still every move was southward with departing summer, and once again I heard with pleasure rumours of repatriation. It might happen any day. As winter approached, there were many attempts to escape from Freiburg, and they seemed to be especially hopeless. There was no barbed wire to break, certainly, in place of it old masonry walls about two feet thick. Sentries were bribed to bring in bars. Most of the rooms had big cupboards, and inside there the sanguine captives got to work. Some were weeks boring patiently and all seemed to conclude that the best plan was to break through the university chapel. In one case, after the prisoners had worked for days, they broke through the wall, only to find a detachment of Germans, wearing carpet slippers, waiting for them to get through.

Many got out of camp, some were very near the frontier when caught, but I can't remember that anyone actually got away. Amongst those who tried and failed was Captain William Robinson VC, who brought down the first Zeppelin in London. There were finally about 80 sentries guarding 250 prisoners, yet attempts to escape continued as long as I remained at Freiburg. Whatever the risk, whatever the consequences, they were prepared to face them if they could get the first two requisites—a map of the border and civilian clothes. The discovery of someone missing was usually made at the first roll call but, if possible, someone else answered. Prison vigilance increased, the sentries paid surprise visits at night to see if all prisoners were in their beds, and more than once were bluffed for the moment with a dummy. It was a complete puzzle to the guards to find a bed vacant in the morning where there had been a sleeping prisoner at midnight. They took no risks afterwards but turned down the blankets, where only a tuft of hair showed, to see if there was also a face attached to it.

Before leaving Karlsruhe I was a Capitalist in dripping, had ten tins of it in reserve, and bread and dripping was a delicacy. But riches are fleeing, my wealth of dripping was not sent on to Freiburg, but went to help the enemy through a lean crisis.

Freiburg was a big military centre for soldiers either on leave or in training. From the infirmary I could see over the streets, and here again one noticed the absence of young men who were not in uniform. How slovenly and woebegone everything and everybody appeared to be!

All at once the weather began to get very cold and we had several heavy falls of snow. In order to keep warm the prisoners spent much of their time in bed. Each bed had a pair of very thin blankets but, by piling our overcoats and other clothing over them, we managed to keep fairly warm.

Amongst the orderlies in hospital was an Irishman who had been taken prisoner early in the war, and spent a good deal of his spare time in cursing Roger Casement, who had come to them on his recruiting tour of Germany. One day another Irish prisoner, he said, struck the renegade, who never visited them again except with an armed guard. This man was sent to Switzerland to be interned there, but as he was always getting drunk and giving trouble they sent him back to Germany.

Amongst prisoners brought to Freiburg were three Indians, two of them Ghurkhas, one a Sikh. The Ghurkhas seemed to trouble little about loss of caste in having meals prepared for them by Germans, but the Sikh was irreconcilable and much upset. The poor fellow seemed to be in the very depths of despair and would beat the walls with his bare hands. Some of the senior British officers went to the Commandant and explained that the Sikh had no wish to cause trouble; that it was a question of religion, and eventually a small room was given him apart from others. The Indians were a source of endless interest to the Germans who had either met or heard of the Ghurkha. They would often show us, in convincing pantomime, how the Ghurkhas, with their big knives in their mouths, stole upon the sentries in the darkness, cut their throats and took away their ears as a 'souvenir'. They thought them terrible fellows.

Freiburg, like many of these old towns of southern Germany, is a really beautiful place. Situated close to the edge of the Black Forest, one could note the deepening of autumn tones in leaves that 'reddened to the fall'. That ripening of the leaf over a whole countryside was a new and rare sight to us Australians, a new study in landscape beauty of which one never tired.

So the summer which I had seen come to life in Germany passed with great glory in gold and chrome and russet browns. Amid all its glory toiled to the last the women workers in city street and field, silent, often solitary, but always constant. If the curse of war had smitten the men of Germany, the curse of Cain had fallen upon its women in endless toil. The women, of course, are both as sewer and harvester no rare sight in Continental fields, and in Germany she is at best a kind of chattel. German men more than once expressed their surprise that Australians should be as absurd as to give women a vote, the same power as men.

We were given two days' notice of another exchange, this time to Heidelberg, another of the famous old university towns in which many Englishmen have finished their education, not only in days just before the war, but right through the last century. It was in this old association that so many of our Victorian towns in Australia, such as Heidelberg and Carlsruhe, got their names.

We were well treated on our journey to Heidelberg, given first-class carriages which had been heated for the journey. It seemed to me that the whole process with prisoners for repatriation was one of thawing out. Commencing with black bitterness that had bitten deep in, we were being given time to change our minds about Germany, so that last impressions should be the best. So in the last stage, the road to old Heidelberg, everything was in apple pie order.

There were very many of the old regular officers both at Freiburg and Heidelberg who had been prisoners since 1914, and had not realised that in the military spirit and practices of England great change has taken place in their absence, that the military caste had, in the great upheaval in contact with wholly new and character-making conditions, lost much of its exclusiveness. Most of them had managed in time to make themselves comfortable with folding beds and trunks of clothes. At Freiburg we had been distributed in different barracks, a few officers of the new army, two of them Australians, being given one long shed. A Colonel of the regulars desired it and gave them a polite hint to clear out, but even a Colonel of the regulars discovered that this was not quite the right way to go about it. Coupled with a lamentable want of veneration for army traditions, he discovered disconcerting gifts in free and easy persiflage, heard the old generation referred to as 'bow and arrow merchants'. Having asserted their right, the juniors allowed the Colonel to have the room.

One of the regulars remarked that I was very young to be a Captain; promotion, he said, seemed to be easy, and mentioned that he had fought in the Boer War.

'It took nearly twenty years to make Captain then,' remarked another officer. 'It only takes thirty dead officers to do it now.'

As there was not enough barrack accommodation at Heidelberg, some of us had to go into leaky huts, through gaps in which the winter wind howled dismally, and they had the additional defect of being dirty. The officials, however, had acquired 'the farewell manner', and were not exacting. In my hut was a Canadian General who had had a sad experience and was mentally broken in consequence. He had been taken at Ypres in 1916, after being rather badly buried by a shell explosion, and seemed to have suffered every torture, including long spells of solitary confinement, that only the malignant German mind could devise. In lucid periods he explained that he knew he was mad, and that the solitary confinement had done it. I began then to see a new significance in my Bochum experience. Any noise seemed to drive the poor fellow frantic, almost every day he seemed to have the impression that something terrible was just about to happen. He had as a special attendant an old Scottish soldier of the regulars, who had obtained great influence over him.

He believed that all the French and Belgian officers had some design against him, and the old soldier would say soothingly, 'Oh, just leave them to me. I'll see that they do no harm.'

Near the camp was an aviation school, and often when passing over the young German cadets used to make a sudden dip at the prisoners to cause a scatter, and play other antics for our confusion and their own diversion. One day something happened. The machine dipped, skimmed close over a group of prisoners, and took the ground just clear of the fence. It taxied for some distance, and then one of the wings struck a tree and went whirling wildly. A roar of cheers broke from a hundred prisoners' throats in appreciation of the collapse. The young aviator was carried in and died soon afterwards. There were no further stunts of that kind. On the day before Christmas a squadron of our machines bombed Mannheim and flew close to Heidelberg, but their formation had then broken up and with heavy anti-aircraft fire it seemed to us that they were able to do little, though the papers next day admitted great damage from the raid.

Ever since October, McQuiggan and I had been saving up some things for a Christmas dinner, amongst the stock being some tinned meat, a Christmas pudding and custard powders. We were asked to dine with another party, so passed over all our supplies. Some good foragers had managed to steal potatoes, and about ten of us had a great spread, roast potatoes being one of the chief luxuries. That evening we were told that on the following day some of us would be leaving for

Switzerland, but I was not particularly overjoyed to find my name in the list, because my Canadian pal was being sent to England a little later. Feeling a 'bit fed up', I complained to the German officials, who assured me that it would be all right. I had a strong feeling, however that it was all wrong. Before leaving Karlsruhe a Scottish flying officer was brought in prisoner. He had got far behind German lines, made an important reconnaissance over Douai, near the French frontier between Lille and Arras. He was most anxious that the information should get back to headquarters as soon as possible, and as it seemed likely that I would be repatriated early, he asked me to take it. To have put anything on paper would be dangerous, so he drew maps of the locality which I could reproduce from memory, and repeated the vital facts until I was quite sure of them. He must have spoken about it outside afterwards, and my impression is that the Germans at least heard enough to be suspicious, and to determine that while they had no reasonable excuse for holding me longer as prisoner, I should not, if it could be managed, reach England. I have already mentioned the fact that in the bag which I had been compelled to leave at Bochum were some very candid notes as to the German treatment of prisoners. I had some uneasy moments when that bag afterwards arrived and was about to be searched by the interpreter. I thought it better in the circumstances to take the bull boldly by the horns.

'You will find in that bag some notes made at Bochum which are not at all complimentary to you. But I was very much down on it then. Don't make too big a mouthful of them.'

'I understand,' he said. 'I won't see or say anything.' So he handed me the papers which, with a feeling of great satisfaction, I at once destroyed. They thought possibly that a few months in Switzerland might help me to forget.

Chapter 21

A Swiss welcome

On the evening of December 27th we got word that we were leaving that night for Switzerland. That we were not going directly home ceased to be a worry any longer. We were at last leaving Germany and all its Teutonic deviltries behind, but taking with us a memory of brutalities so bitter that they are never likely to be obliterated. We started late at night when Heidelberg was mostly a-bed, and those who were fit to do so marched through the keen, clear winter night to the railway station and were entrained about midnight. It was appropriate that we should leave Hunland in darkness, for in darkness we had found it. And what a change in the enemy attitude! We were 'sir'-ed and saluted at every turn, nothing was too good for the dear departing. First class carriages were at our disposal, all so wonderfully heated that, in spite of the snow, we were obliged in a little while to turn off the heaters and open the windows. Germany was doing us well. But the reformation came rather late. The pet epithet of 'swine-hound' will (without the hound) always typify to me the German character. If they are much accustomed to use that phrase to each other, it has been mostly wisely chosen. Swine is their stock food, and one wondered at times whether, on the doctrine of 'Like begets like', some qualities of the animal had become absorbed in their national nature and fibre.

At seven in the morning we reached the breakfast station, and found the meal waiting for us, meat in abundance, a big ration of bread, two bowls of coffee (over-sweetened) and lots of milk. It was a good meal, although they charged us five shillings for it. Arriving at Constance, which is half-Swiss, half-German, they took us to a restaurant for another meal and a fat one. The Hun was even painfully anxious to make a good last impression, but he doesn't give away good impressions; he sells them. For the last meal in Germany they charged us six shillings, and on market values it was worth the money. As we were taken down to the station the officials said anxiously, 'We showed you every consideration, did we not?'

On our side, even in those moments of full hearted thankfulness, not many compliments were wasted. They were so very obviously hedging on 'the wrath to come'. The whole thing was a significant demonstration of German doubt as to the future, and their personal and particular relation to it. When the Swiss train pulled out of the station there was no longer a German official in sight, only Swiss soldiers and Red Cross men. 'Mum's the word' was the message passed along as the train started. We had asked the Swiss officials to let us know when the train crossed the frontier, and on the instant a yell, which by this time must be familiar to the ears of Constance, rose from the prison train. In that yell were mixed up many emotions. If it said anathema to all things German, it had some of the spirit if not the form of a hymn of thanksgiving. The frantic cheering lasted long, and at every station there were crowds of Swiss people who joined in whole-heartedly.

I shall never forget that demonstration in which people of many nations joined, for Switzerland is at once the home, the halting place, the holiday Mecca of many nations. French, English, Americans and Swiss seemed to compete with each other as to which of them could do most for us. Flowers and food were showered upon us. It was not surprising perhaps that, at the large stations where so many of our countrymen assembled, this cordiality should be shown. What surprised and pleased us was that it was repeated at every little Swiss hamlet by the way. People flocked to the station, to the railside and cheered us wildly. There was nothing formal or half-hearted in it, and the Swiss people know how to cheer, though the Briton is often diffident about letting himself go. It takes a very big thing to move him to the depths. So it went on, and well into the night the crowds still came to cheer. It was the happy pilgrimage, shouts of '*Vive la France!*' alternating with '*Vive la Angleterre!*' I learned something afterwards as to the inner meaning of that demonstration.

At about 3 am the train reached Berne, and in spite of the awkwardness of the hour, the British Ambassador, Sir Horace Rumbold, who, with the military attaché, was responsible for the exchange of British prisoners, was there to welcome us. We were at once taken to the station restaurant for the first sumptuous meal we had had for a long time, and many more questions were asked at the moment than were actually answered. We were too busy to speak. In the midst of it all the thought came to many minds—'what if some mistake were made, someone realised an error; who would have to be sent back again?' If that had occurred, there were few on board that train who would not, as a last favour, have asked his best friend to lend him a revolver.

At table those who waited on us were lady volunteers, and looking back now I realised with some feeling of shame that they must have considered us surly beasts. It had more the air of a procession of heroes than the coming home of maimed, wasted, useless prisoners of war, for, of course, only those came out whose fighting days were obviously over. But the hand grips were very real, the welcome wholehearted, and to us it was all overpoweringly, humanly beautiful, the liberty, the good fellowship, the forethought anticipating every wish, a passing from Purgatory to Paradice.

I was taken at once to Montreux, 'the Nice of Switzerland', and surely one of the most lovely spots in all the world, here in winter a wonderland of mountain, lake, cloud and snow, and holding for an Englishman many associations with the past. There Byron, in his pilgrimage, lived a while and wrote, and in his 'Sonnet to Lake Leman' spoke of other immortals:

> To them thy banks were lovely as to all,
> But they have made them lovelier, for the lore
> Of mighty minds doth hallow in the core
> Of human hearts the ruin of a wall
> Where dwelt the wise and wondrous; but by thee
> How much more, Lake of Beauty! do we feel,
> In sweetly gliding o'er thy crystal sea,
> The wild glow of that not ungentle zeal,
> Which of the heirs of immortality
> Is proud, and makes the breath of glory real!

At Montreux, where we arrived early in the afternoon, we were further welcomed, the crowd thronged not only the platform, but the street outside, and passing through to the hotel we were showered in flowers, although it was midwinter. It was all just wonderful. At the Swiss hotel were bands of music, a big dinner and little speeches. My uniform was still nondescript, my only footwear a pair of well-worn carpet slippers. It was cold, but the scarecrows were very happy. After the welcome we were taken in cars to our hotels, glad to settle down to the new life for a time, because after the great excitement came reaction. In Switzerland one was never given time to be unhappy, so many splendid people we met, all anxious to show us kindness. Cards and invitations floated in, many more invitations that one could possible accept, even if he were a cripple with the 'Go slow!' warning before his eyes.

At Montreux many things happened that helped to happiness. There was the friendship of the Doubledays, who insisted that I must come to them when I pleased, make their place my home. I knew that it was no mere invitation or courtesy, that they wished it and I knew how much I wanted it. Then there was a letter from my dear father in Australia with the news of home, again a letter from Colonel Wiltshire of my old corps, which I quote here for one reason only. I have mentioned the mortification of being taken prisoner. The thought had always been with me. 'What will the Battalion think of it?' That haunting trouble rarely left me, even in my worst days in Germany. I knew that I had done fairly well, even amongst gallant company, but knew very well too, that all good service would be washed out in the hard fact of my being taken prisoner. I might have shot myself on the night I fell, but would not have done so even had I thought of it before my revolver was thrown away, because I felt quite sure that I was done. And, but for the Germans, I would have been done. Their assurance that I would die helped more than anything else to bring about the obstructive fighting mood.

If they wanted to be rid of me and of trouble, they went the wrong way about it. There was always little consolation in the thought that at worst I was quits. Even while their machine-gun bullets combed our hair, and their bombs fell all about us, I had landed a grenade, a beauty right amongst them, and it was a Mills bomb, not 'substitute'. The surgeons in Switzerland all expressed wonder that I was alive. I knew exactly how and why. But there was always that thought of the regiment and what it thought, so that Colonel Wiltshire's letter brought peace of mind.

'You may rest assured,' he said, 'that our thoughts have often been with you. I don't know whether you got my last letter, but let me once more say that what you did in that stunt was splendid. You did all that was humanly possible. As far as your reputation and your record go you may rest assured that there is no officer of whom the old regiment is more proud than they are of Billy Cull. Their only regret is that you have not a medal ribbon to show.'

What a relief to know that I still had the regard of those splendid comrades!

Another big element in my happiness at Montreux was renewing the valued friendship with my old friend, Captain Hall. It was all these blessings coming in a heap that helped me more than anything else to make light of my misfortunes. One day, as I made joking reference to my wounds, the dear old Captain burst into tears, then threw his arms about me and fairly hugged me. Many poets have exalted love, but is there after all any sentiment that stands higher than true, disinterested friendship! That I should be so cheerful seemed at Montreux to be a matter for general wonder. One complimentary lady wished to paint me as 'Saint-Somebody'. Now, I ask you? She couldn't know, of course, that whenever thoughts of mine travelled to the other side of the Rhine they were not fit for Saint Anybody. And, if she felt that way, there was no scarcity of suitable subjects. There were many angels in Switzerland.

Between times and kind people there was much to see. The Château de Chillon, famous in song and story, was only a train-ride distant. Byron's Isle was under one's eye: from Glion there was a far and fair look over a romantic winterland.

Here, if it were from common gratitude alone, I would wish to say a word more about the Doubleday family, of their goodness to every poor, battered, derelict Australian they chanced to meet. Miss Leila Doubleday was in Vienna when war broke out, and for a considerable time could not get away. As the guest of a well-known Austrian family, she was not interned, but was under surveillance, and had to report constantly to the police. It was mainly through the good offices of the American Consul that, after many disappointments, she finally reached Switzerland, where she played constantly for soldiers interned there on exchange from Germany, and also for Red Cross movements. In conversation I found that Miss Doubleday, though often in Germany, never liked the people, mainly because of their hostility to everything English, which was manifest long before the war. That Germany turns art, as well as every other artifice, to one absorbing purpose, was apparently in Switzerland during the war, and German propaganda there, Miss Doubleday assured me, was very active indeed. They sent down their best orchestras, sometimes one hundred and twenty players, whole opera companies, to give performances, the proceeds being generously distributed amongst Swiss charities. Leading artists told Miss Doubleday that it was all being paid for by the Government. Their art interest in Switzerland was so absorbing, even in the turmoil of war that they sent along many of the best paintings from their national collections to be exhibited. For a time they had the field to themselves, then the French challenged and beat them at their own game. Leading British and American residents in Switzerland were very anxious that a good dramatic company should be sent out from England to produce the most popular of Shakespeare's plays, but the authorities were averse to propaganda in this form. In Switzerland Miss Doubleday was approached with a proposal for concerts in company with a very celebrated German pianist, but promptly declined the association. Art, it is said, has no nationality, but the German was rather too obvious and odious, even in Switzerland, to be a desirable colleague. Miss Doubleday's brother, Kingsley, for whose sake they were staying in Switzerland, was a painter, but unfortunately an invalid. Her grandmother, Mrs Watson, was one of the best Australians I had ever chanced to meet. Switzerland, she would admit, was a very nice country in small patches. 'But, oh, for my big, beautiful Australia!'

Chapter 22

Old battle grounds

I had been about three weeks in Switzerland when the penalty for all the excitement came in a complete nervous breakdown. It lasted for about three weeks, during the greater part of which I was unable either to sleep or read. The heart-beats kept up in the neighbourhood of 92, about twenty over normal, and I have the strongest conviction that it was chiefly the tender devoted nursing of Mrs Doubleday and her family that pulled me through.[29]

Although at the outbreak of war the sympathies of the Swiss people were largely with their near neighbour, the Bosche, all that has changed, and the change came long before it was evident that Germany was beaten, so it is not quite a case of shouting with the biggest crowd. It was mainly the atrocities and infamies of the Bosche that first turned them against him, the convincing evidence that Germany was the enemy of the smaller nations, whose cause France and Britain championed. Of the two it is undoubtedly France whom they most love and respect. Yet at a New Year function to which we were invited, a Swiss Captain in eulogising the Allies especially singles out Britain, and referred at length to Australians. At and after Gallipoli the Swiss people, he said, began to regard the Australians as altogether a new type of men. He mentioned that before hostilities commenced there were enquiries from Germany as to what would be the attitude of Switzerland, if Germany wished to send an army across their territory. The reply was that they would resent it.

'And if 200 000 men are sent along with application?'

'We have 300 000 men to say "No" to it, and they all fire bullets from their rifles.'

The point of that last observation is that the Swiss claim to be the finest rifle shots in the world, and are especially proud of their reputation. We were told in confidence that they would not be at all surprised if the Germans, even as late as the beginning of 1918, tried to force a passage, and the Swiss professed to be quite ready for the contingency.

Their position as an isolated buffer State is peculiar, since for so many things, the essentials of everyday life and work, they are absolutely dependent on neighbour nations. France largely supplies them with meat and wheat in exchange for milk, chocolate and goods of that sort. For coal and timber they are wholly dependent on Germany, and the Hun, always looking ahead, was careful never to let them accumulate large reserve stocks of either. In the event of war, the Swiss railways would be at a standstill in about a fortnight. Just before I left Switzerland there was some trouble about deserters, largely Russian, German and Italian, who had taken sanctuary. The Socialists, who are apparently strong, sent a demand to the Swiss Federal Council that these deserters should not be compelled to work, as they were the guests of the country. The demand was ignored; the council insisted that they should work, and in one district at least the deserters, chiefly Russian, armed themselves with old scythes and weapons of that kind to resist the ordinance. Garrison troops were immediately called out and sent to the affected districts, and on the first sight of them the Russians threw down their weapons and went to work.

The district between Montreux and Lausanne was a Socialist stronghold. I was told that both Lenin and Trotsky lived there at one time, and it was from there that, in co-operation with Germany, they worked up the revolution.

After I had been more than once x-rayed by Swiss surgeons, one of whom stands in the forefront of the profession, they told me that nothing could be done. All the right hip bone had been blown away, including the socket, and the femur was too short. I suggested amputation, but the surgeon said, 'Oh no; that would kill you!'

As an indication of Swiss feeling in the war, the street hoardings were illuminative. It was quite a common thing to see such a rough inscription as *'Bosche sale cochon'* which meant 'dirty pigs'. There was a big German contingent in Switzerland, official and otherwise, and the rival camps did not mix. The majority of the Swiss seemed to take it as a settled fact that the Kaiser was mad. In referring to atrocities they mentioned the *Lusitania* crime, which the Germans pleaded was justifiable as a war measure. It was in Switzerland that I first saw one of the medals struck in Germany to celebrate the sinking of the *Lusitania*.

On New Year's Eve, having been out at a party, I was hobbling back to my hotel when I came upon a party of Swiss youths, who, on seeing me, make a rush, got around me on every side, and insisted upon shaking hands, while they shouted, *'Vive l'Angleterre!'* They praised the British, who, they said, were fighting a Swiss as well as an English war, escorted me home, and finished up with, 'God Save the King.' Then they marched off, singing 'It's a long way to Tipperary.'

The chief conditions of internment were restriction to an area within five miles of the billet, and we were supposed to be in by midnight. It was a request that we should stay at one hotel, and if one wished for any reason to leave the area he made application to the Swiss authorities, and had no difficulty in obtaining leave for three days and two nights. A Swiss Board, having considered German reports upon any case, was given the right to say whether prisoners should remain there or be repatriated to England. All interned prisoners of war, in moving about, got concession tickets both by rail and tram, at half the usual cost. The wounded were both publicly and privately shown every possible consideration. If you wished to enter a tram the passengers would jump down to assist you, and where there was no room available both men and women stood up to offer you a choice of seats. In railway trains it was the same—everyone very thoughtful and courteous. The impression one got was that Switzerland enjoyed greater social equality, fewer class distinctions than any other land I have known. That applied to those who were wholly Swiss. In the very large resident French colony, where the parentage on both sides was French, the social code was more noticeable.

The amazing thing to me was that everybody seemed to be able to speak English, and took special pride in the accomplishment. That is no doubt an outcome and a necessity of the tourist business, in which so many are interested. All the stores had three prices for their goods: the lowest for their own people, a higher charge for all the tourists, a third charge, highest of all, for the British officer. The British officer of the old school generally had money to burn and no hesitation about burning it. He never priced things, so paid more than anybody else. As the interned soldier colony grew, the casino was started for the officers again, but many of them gambled so heavily and continuously that it was soon declared 'out of bounds'. By this time a good many who saw and suffered out the war in German compounds have discovered that a great many affections and habits of old days went into the melting-pot in their absence, and that even the rich must find a new a practical purpose in life, will be relieved from the old mental distress of killing time. In another way it was almost time that the casino was closed down, for the bank was having much the better of the deal in chances. One shop paid eight to one; then they reduced it to seven to one, making it, by mathematical law, a certainty for themselves.

It is not realised, perhaps, that during the war and because of it the Swiss were rationed in bread, butter and fats. The allowance of bread, 225 grams, was enough, but the ration of butter was frugal, and at the restaurants a very tiny pat was served with afternoon tea. Cakes made of potato meal were particularly good, and these could be got without a ration card, while one might buy as many rusks as he pleased—at a price. All goods were dear. For a pair of brown walking boots I paid £2/10/−.

With many of us compound habits became so fixed that, for days after we reached Switzerland, prisoners sitting patiently in their rooms suddenly realised, with a gasp of astonishment, that they were free to go outside. It took several days to accustom myself to liberty, to remember that there was no sentry and no barbed wire blocking the way.

Another strange experience came in relation to pain. In Germany I was never free from pain, at first a pain so intense, so agonising that, coupled with the long solitary confinement I had an ever-present horror of it driving me mad. There was always the consciousness of a double fight at Bochum, one for recovery, one for reason. As the wounds improved, began to close, and the pain decreased, I often found myself at night unable to sleep, and suddenly realised the reason. I was not in pain, and I needed pain, liked a little of it, so I would press upon my shattered leg, get some pain, and then fall asleep. When I mentioned this to a member of the Swiss Medical Board for interned prisoners, and added 'I suppose you will call me a fool,' he said, 'Oh no; pain has grown upon you, has become a habit, just like the morphia.'

In going finally before the Medical Board, I understood that both legs must be 'dud' before one had any chance of repatriation, so was naturally anxious. Several of those examined before me had to strip, but when it came to my turn the senior medical officer said, 'Oh! This is Captain Cull. You need not strip Captain.'

While being examined I asked whether I should mention the wounds received on Gallipoli.

'Oh, not at all Captain Cull. The only thing that worries us is that your injuries are so very bad.'

When the Board rose, Dr Chasse kindly came down in his car to say that I was one of two out of thirteen applicants passed for repatriation to England. In one sense only the decision was discouraging, because no prisoner was sent to England if it were possible to do anything for him in Switzerland. In consumption cases it was much better, of course, that they should remain in Switzerland, whatever their desires might be; but, apart from such special cases, it seemed to me that there was an understanding that as many wounded as possible should for the time be kept in Switzerland, English war hospitals being, without much doubt, overcrowded.

By coincidence I left Switzerland on the very day that the great German offensive in northern France began, the long stern battle which few of us then realised was the end in the utter defeat and downfall of the Hun. There was a great crowd to see us off, bands playing and much cheering, so that my first and last impressions of Switzerland were warmed by that friendly fervour which mellows even misfortune. Crossing the frontier into France, we were transferred to a British hospital train, and so went by way to Dijon, Amiens—which later was one of the pivotal points of the great battle, the scene of undying glory to Australian arms—Abbeville to Boulogne.

Amiens, on the old fighting front, completed a circle of many emotions. It was strange to find oneself just where he had begun, saddening to realise that in the great struggle impending he could no longer lend a hand. There was all the old cruel signs of a Hun offensive, the fugitives flocking south again, crowding the roads; old men, old women, children, all the unhappy martyrs of France, and every conceivable sort of vehicle from wheelbarrows to country carts. The genial spring which, with its new leafage, was to bring new hope for Europe, had yet to come. It was winter, and my heart ached for those unhappy victims of war who had gone forward at the heels of their armies to reoccupy their old homes only to find that once again they must trek for refuge—whether they knew it or not. There was nothing in that sad spectacle to reassure one as to the early dawn of victory. The civilians came one way, toiling slowly through mud and rain; in the other direction, often it seemed in hopeless congestion, went the troop trains with singing soldiers. No doubts or doleful imaginings there! The British soldiers, and they seemed to be almost all British, were flocking forward to throw themselves, as at Mons, against the foam of the second great German wave that was sweeping over France, and they went to hobnob with death as merrily as if he were Father Christmas and theirs a holiday excursion.

Had I but known what was to come, no bit of that battle smitten country about Amiens would have been overlooked. I would have tried to make such a mental map of it as would last through the life of a man, and in the history of his country endure forever. Perhaps I looked upon that very spot where our divisions passed through the broken lines of French and British never, until they reached the Rhine, to look behind them again. There was nothing obvious then, but the sign of a great struggle, and, for the moment, an uncertain end. Only that Master Strategist, who held in his hands all the threads of far-flung battle, could have given us the hopeful word.

Next to all the great signs, men flocking to battle as doves to the windows, and the continuous, distant rumble of that cannon fire once so familiar, I noticed the novelty of the little things, the abundance of white bread, of butter, all those ordinary things of life which to a prisoner had become important and unusual.

We thought we had been well fed, well cared for in a neutral country, until we realised the splendid fare of the hospital trains, the care and companionship of the nursing sisters, so sympathetic, so beautiful. Had we not been prisoners of war we would have taken it all as a matter of course, part of the privileges we were entitled to expect, but being what we were, knowing what we knew, it was all wonderful.

At about ten o'clock at night we arrived at Boulogne, and had barely reached the station when the air raid alarm sounded. We had not yet lost touch of war. The German Gotha bombers came over in relays, and for about two hours, bombed the French port heavily, while we sat in the train as onlookers. Shrapnel from the aircraft guns was showering all about us. Two heavy bombs dropped on the line within a short distance of the train. I was looking out of the window at the time, and the blast of the bomb seemed to take my scalp off, so that I impulsively grabbed at my head with both hands. It was all there. As a matter of fact, nothing had come near me, but the force of the explosion seemed to set the old Gallipoli wounds tingling, and for a time my head felt peculiarly hot. As soon as 'Raid off' sounded we were placed in ambulances and taken to the convalescent home, where there was another cordial reception and all sorts of kind treatment. Early next morning the ambulances took us to the boat, and without any event of interest we were landed in Dover.

Here this story properly ends. The home coming was saddened somewhat by the early consciousness that there were still too many eligibles drifting about. I could not forget that, amongst my brother fighting at the front, 'The Kiddy', too young to be accepted when war broke out, had been ten months in the trenches. As one of the recruiting staff who sought day after day to make men realise their duty, redeem their honour, one sickened often before the conviction that far too many Australians had neither visualised the war nor realised their own obligations. To have been one in that great companionship of Anzac and afterwards is full compensation for suffering. I have heard a hundred men, broken in body but not in spirit, say that it was worth all the suffering of the past, all the pain of the future, to have been with them, to have realised the Australian as a century of peace could never have discovered him. The task to which he put his hand is done.

> *Not once or twice in our fair island-story*
> *The path of duty was the way to glory.*
> *He, that ever following her commands,*
> *On with toil of heart and knees and hands,*
> *Thro' the long gorge to the far light has won*
> *His path upward, and prevail'd,*
> *Shall find the topping crags of Duty scaled*
> *Are close upon the shining table-lands*
> *To which our God Himself is moon and sun.*

THE END

Epilogue

Under the provisions of the 1907 Hague Convention, Germany, Britain and France agreed that all sick and wounded prisoners of war unable to resume active service were to be considered for exchange to a neutral country. Amputees, the blind, the physically impaired, the mentally ill and men suffering from tuberculosis were all candidates for exchange. Prisoners who felt they might be eligible for internment had a right to go before a panel of Swiss and German physicians for examination. For thousands of wounded and sick prisoners of war attempting to leave Germany, going before the repatriation commission was an exercise filled with anxiety and sometimes disappointment. But the severity of Cull's wounds meant that he was approved for exchange and on 28 December 1917 he and Lieutenant McQuiggan were among the first wounded Australian prisoners to cross the German border into neutral Switzerland as part of the exchange agreement. Cull had survived his ordeal in German prison camps but lasted just four months interned at the Hotel de l'Europe at Montreux before his health began to deteriorate. He was sent to England in March 1918 and after two weeks of treatment at Millbank Hospital in London, was put on a troopship and repatriated to Australia. He was just 24 when he was discharged from the AIF in his home state of Victoria in October 1918.

Capture had prevented Cull from any further fighting and perhaps spared him from being killed in later actions, but it also stalled any further career in the AIF. Despite his bravery on numerous occasions, Cull was among the very few infantry officers who had served at Gallipoli and the Western Front who ended the war without decoration for leadership or gallantry. Cull claimed he was not a 'decoration hunter' but from the letter he received from his commanding officer, Colonel Aubrey Wiltshire, we get in the impression that Cull was recommended for the Military Cross but for one reason or another had missed out—not because his deeds were not gallant enough, but because units possessed a limited number of decorations that could only go to the most outstanding actions. In February 1917, just two weeks before his capture, Cull was recommended for the Italian Silver Medal for Military Valour for 'conspicuous gallantry in the execution of repeated reconnaissances in No Man's Land at Fleurbaix and Armentières' but was captured before the recommendation was approved.[30]

The following month, the War Office issued instructions that precluded prisoners of war from being considered for an award if the act for which they were recommended was in any way associated with their capture.[31] This order prevented Cull from being decorated for his actions in relation to the attack on Malt Trench, although the letter from Colonel Wilshire suggests that Cull was most certainly deserving of one. These instructions were overruled by amendments made in May 1919 so that prisoners of war who made examples of themselves by caring for the sick and wounded or attempting to escape could be considered for decoration.[32] Cull was too injured to even think about escaping let alone attempt one, and received no further commendation. In 1923 the Department of Defence issued Cull with the three campaign medals he was entitled to wear—the 1914/15 Star, the British War Medal, and the Victory Medal.

Little is known about William Cull after his repatriation to Australia and how he fared afterwards, but it is beyond doubt that the war and his disability shaped the remainder of his days. Few historical records document Cull's post-war life, but we know that he became involved in the Returned Soldiers Sailors Imperial League of Australia (RSSILA) in Melbourne and was one of the Victorian representatives of the Repatriation Commission around the same time he became passionate about state politics. Cull was the nationalist candidate for the seat of Albert Park in the Victorian Legislative Assembly by-election in November 1919, but was defeated by the Labour nominee Arthur Wallace by 733 votes.[33] There are no further references to Cull's aspiring political career other than he was forced to retire early due to ill-health. We know that he married Ms Dorris Whitgelaw in 1920, became a father to Elsa the following year, and the Cull family lived at Brighton Beach in Melbourne's south east. Cull paraded with the 46th Battalion (The Brighton Rifles), Citizens Military Force, until 1928. By the mid-1930s William Cull was working as the managing editor of *The Shepparton Advertiser* while his family resided at Chelsea, but little is known regarding how the family coped in the years of the Great Depression.[34]

The ongoing effects of his wounds received in action at Malt Trench in February 1917 dogged Cull for the remainder of his days. On Saturday 20 August 1939, he suffered a massive heart attack at his mother's 80th birthday party in Preston as he stood up to respond to a toast. Aged just 44, he died before medical attention could be administered. He was buried at a modest service at the family vault at Coburg Cemetery, where a bugler sounded the Last Post.[35]

Notes

1   Records Section, AIF Headquarters, *Australian Imperial Force: statistics of casualties*, (London: Records Section, AIF Headquarters, 1919), p. 15.

2   C.E.W. Bean, *Official history of Australia in the war of 1914–1918*, Vol. IV, 6th ed., (Sydney: Angus & Robertson, 1938), p. 342–343; C.E.W. Bean, 'Punishing Australians: German treatment of our countrymen', *Commonwealth Gazette*, 29 October 1917, p. 2809.

3   A. G. Butler, *Official history of the Australian Army Medical Services in the war of 1914–1918*, 1st ed., (Sydney: Angus & Robertson, 1943), pp. 896–897.

4   William Cull was the second youngest of four brothers. Cecil, the eldest, enlisted in August 1915 and served

with the 8th Battalion for the duration of the war; Joseph enlisted in January 1916 and served with the 10th Field Company Engineers; and the youngest brother, Robert, enlisted in September 1916 and served with the 37th Battalion. Later referred to by Cull as 'the Kiddy', Robert was awarded the Military Medal for carrying an important message to company headquarters at Heilly while under heavy artillery and machine gun fire during the German spring offensive on 28 March 1918.

5   Cull's experiences as a scouting officer appear in the official records held at the Australian War Memorial. This particular patrol is mentioned in the War Diary of the 23rd Battalion, AWM4 23/40/70, April 1916, p. 8.

6   Private Charles Johnson, 23rd Battalion, was awarded the Military Medal for work as a stretcher bearer during the 5th Brigade's attack at Pozières on 29 July 1916.

7   The Germans encountered during this raid were of the 230th *Reserve Infanterie Regiment* of the 50th (Prussian) Reserve Division. They were a familiar adversary of the Australian troops who encountered them at Mouquet Farm in August 1916, Polygon Wood in September 1917, Broodseinde in October 1917, and at Dernancourt in April 1918.

8   The 6th Brigade's raid on the night of 29/30 June 1916 was considered a successful enterprise: in total, the three Australian battalions that took part in the raid captured five prisoners but had killed at least eighty at the expense of

seven of their own killed and fifteen wounded. The efforts of Cull and the officer leading the 23rd Battalion raiding party, Captain Hugh Conran, were both mentioned in the battalion's routine orders. For more, see Charles Bean, *Official history of Australia in the war of 1914–1918*, Vol. III, (Sydney: Angus & Robertson, 1929), pp. 266–270; AWM4, 23/40/9, 23rd Battalion War Diary, June 1916, p.10; AWM4 23/6/01, 6th Brigade War Diary, June 1916, p. 13.

9   Sergeant William John Gordon Graham, 23rd Battalion, was evacuated to England two weeks after suffering gunshot wounds to his chest and arm. He slowly recovered from his wounds, and for his part in the raid was awarded the Military Medal. He was repatriated to Australia in July 1917.

10 It is more than likely that this man was 1737 Private Frank Jones, 23rd Battalion, who enlisted under a pseudonym rather than his real name, Francis James Cordwell. Jones later transferred to the 22nd Battalion and was awarded the Military Medal for actions as a stretcher bearer at Pozières on the night of 4/5 August 1916. He survived the war and returned to Australia in March 1919, but died soon after.

11 Donington Hall was a manor house and estate near Derby in North West Leicestershire that was requisitioned by the British government on the outbreak of war and converted into a camp for German prisoners. Its luxurious environs

caused much debate in the British press about whether or not it was appropriate to hold German prisoners of war. Conditions were good and prisoners were well treated, and the gulf between the Western Front and Donington Hall was immense.

12 For this action and for 'energetic and able work' during the attack on 28/29 July 1916 Captain Robert Maberly Smith, 23rd Battalion, was awarded the Military Cross.

13 Cull is referring to the 27th Battalion and its attack on Bayonet Trench on 5 November 1916. The Battalion succeeded in breaking into the German position, but like many parts of the line in that sector, it was merely a series of connected shell holes. Rifles clogged with mud and a bomb fight ensued, but owing to a shortage of ammunition the Australian attackers were forced to retire by a much stronger German opponent. Charles Bean, the Australian official historian, documents in the *Official history* that the troops encountered during this action were troops of the 4th Guard Division, which unlike the Australians, had been sufficiently rested after fighting on the Somme. Seventy-seven Australians were killed, 141 were wounded and 75 were missing. Eight men were taken prisoner of war in this action, of which three succumbed to their wounds in German captivity.

14 This last comment refers to the 'scorched earth' policy adopted by the German Army in February 1917 as it began withdrawing from the Somme in order to take up

stronger defensive positions along the heavily fortified Hindenburg Line in the Arras sector. Codenamed 'Albericht', the Germans destroyed roads, villages, towns and wells so that the advancing British Army would have a hard time establishing strong points from which to launch attacks against the new German positions. French inhabitants of the area were transferred to towns and cities under German occupation, and much of their property was destroyed. The policy further undermined the German Army's credibility that it was adhering to the Hague Convention. According to Charles Bean, the policy 'strengthened the legend of Teutonic brutality which so greatly harmed the German cause both during and after the war.'

15 A veteran of the Boer War, Captain Arthur Kennedy, 23rd Battalion, was picked up by German troops after being wounded in the ankle by shrapnel following the 6th Brigade's ill-fated attack on the OG lines at Pozières on 28/29 July 1916. He is listed as having as died of pneumonia at Göttingen less than a month later, but accounts by repatriated Australian prisoners suggest that this may not have been the case. According to one man's statement, the state of Kennedy's wounds necessitated the amputation of his leg at a German field hospital and he died soon after.

16 Private Sydney Shearn, 22nd Battalion, was among thirty-three Australians taken prisoner during the

Second Battle of Bullecourt on 5 May 1917. Shearn was wounded in the hand during the action, and like Cull, his injuries were severe enough to warrant a transfer from Germany to Switzerland where he spent the remainder of the war. He was repatriated to England in December 1918.

17 According to the 6th Brigade War Diary, the 21st and 22nd Battalions attacked Malt Trench at 17.30. Some field guns of 2nd Divisional Artillery had already been moved up the line but were either registering targets elsewhere, were bogged in mud, or were sitting on railway cars waiting to be moved up the line. Orders for all guns on the V Army front to be brought forward was not received until 17.45—fifteen minutes after the attack on Malt Trench had begun. AWM4 23/6/18, 6th Brigade, February 1917, p. 9; AWM4 13/11/12, 2nd Divisional Artillery, February 1917, p. 5.

18 Private Claude Martin was killed at Second Bullecourt on 5 May 1917, but unknown to Cull, Lieutenant William Corne was killed during the attack on Malt Trench that night. Both men are among 10,765 Australians listed on the Australian national memorial at Villers-Bretonneux who were killed in action or died of wounds on the battlefields of northern France and have no known grave.

19 Lieutenant Karl Ahnall DCM, 28th Battalion, was captured during the 7th Brigade's attack on Malt Trench on 28 February 1917.

20   A *Lager* is a prisoner of war camp.

21   Records of the Australian Red Cross Society held at the
Australian War Memorial document how convoluted
the notification process was, mainly because all
correspondence to and from Germany passed through
neutral Holland. For Cull, official notification of his
status as a prisoner of war took months. A postcard
written by someone other than Cull was sent from St
Elizabeth's Hospital at Bochum on 30 March, arriving at
the Australian Red Cross Wounded and Missing Bureau
in London on 10 May. This was the first news that Cull
had not been killed in action, as had been suspected,
but he was in fact a prisoner of war in Germany: 'Will
you kindly send me a parcel of food and clothes etc.
I have been a prisoner of war for about 5 weeks now,
and would be much obliged if you could despatch the
kit, shaving stuff I want badly'. On 1 April, Cull himself
wrote a note to the Australian Red Cross sounding far
more desperate than the unknown author of the previous
message: 'I receive no parcels, so beg that you forward
me parcels according to the scheme you have in hand'.
Eyewitnesses of the 22nd Battalion reported last seeing
Cull seriously wounded near the German wire at Malt
Trench, but news of his current state of health did not
reach the Australian Red Cross until two weeks after
they had received his note of 1 April. Why he made no
mention of his wounds in his previous correspondence

is unknown. Cull's platoon sergeant in France received a letter from him later that month stating that he was 'Seriously Wounded and a Prisoner of War in Germany', and based on this information, the Wounded and Missing Bureau of the Australian Red Cross unofficially informed Cull's next of kin in Australia that their son was alive but seriously wounded. To help alleviate any further suffering that Cull may have been enduring in Germany, food parcels from the office of the Australian Prisoner of War Department in London were immediately dispatched to his return address at Bochum. The Australian Red Cross received official notification from Berlin several days later that Cull was a prisoner of war. By then, a sorely needed relief package was already on its way. Just as time consuming and convoluted was the postal system, which could not be relied upon by prisoners for urgent requests of food and clothing. There is no evidence to suggest that the letter Cull was so proud of writing to his family ever reached England, although this was not uncommon. British prisoners in Germany were permitted to write one letter a month and one postcard weekly, which were then sent on to England, via Holland, every ten days. All correspondence had to be written in pencil and had to pass examination by a team of German translators and censors attached to the administration office at each prisoner of war camp or hospital. If the letter was longer than the prescribed length, or it disclosed information unrelated to the sender's personal affairs—such as inadequate conditions or deliberate mistreatment—it was either returned for amendment or destroyed without the sender's knowledge. News from prisoners in Germany could literally take months. AWMIDRL/0428, Australian Red Cross Society, Prisoner of War Department, Captain W. A. Cull, 22nd Battalion.

22 This was a standard procedure in all prison camps in Germany. All packages had to be opened and examined in the presence of the prisoner at the censorship office for forbidden correspondence or items that could be used for the purposes of escape. This extended to tinned foods, much to the resentment of the prisoners, which also had to be opened and searched for contraband.

23 Here Cull is referring to the typhus epidemics at the 'horror' camps of Gardelegan and Wittenberg between late 1914 and early 1915. In the first year of the war, the German government refused requests to place prisoners of different nationalities in separate camps on the basis that they were all part of the Entente and fighting a war against Germany. Sanitary conditions in the two camps were poor, the camps were overcrowded, the prisoners were undernourished and the winter was bitterly cold. Russian prisoners who had lived with the disease on the Eastern Front transmitted it amongst the British, French and Belgians, causing a deadly epidemic of high

fever, delirium, bodily weakness and in some cases, gangrene. In fear that the disease spread any further, the German guard and military authorities vacated both camps and left the administration up to the prisoners of war. There were between 200 and 300 cases amongst British prisoners at Wittenburg, of which sixty died of disease.

24   Despite the popularity of escape stories on film and in print, few attempts at making a bold bid for freedom succeeded. Of the 3861 Australians taken prisoner on the Western Front and imprisoned in Germany, only forty-three were successful in making their way to friendly territory. War office, *Statistics of the Military effort of the British Empire during the Great War, 1914–1920*, (London: HMSO, 1922), p.329.

25   Cologne was spared serious damage by aerial bombing during the First World War, but was subjected to no less than 262 raids by RAF Bomber Command and the USAAF Eighth Air Force during the Second World War. On the night of 30 May 1942, Air Chief Marshall Arthur Harris, Commander in Chief of RAF Bomber Command, launched a raid on Cologne with over 1000 bombers as a demonstration to the British public that area bombing could bring Nazi Germany to its knees. In what has become a highly controversial raid against a target with no clear military objective, 3300 homes were destroyed and 1200 people were killed.

26 Following this transaction, the American Express Company notified the Australian Red Cross that Cull had made a withdrawal at Karlsruhe. Fortunately, official notification that Cull had been transferred from St Elizabeth's hospital at Bochum had been received from Berlin two weeks earlier and a Red Cross food parcel was making its way to Karlsruhe. AWMIDRL/0428, ARCS POW Dept, Capt. W. A. Cull.

27 McQuiggin was one of 1170 Australians taken prisoner during the First Battle of Bullecourt on 11 April 1917.

28 Captain Frederick Hoad, 7th Battalion, was seriously wounded by shrapnel and captured at Mouquet Farm on 18 August 1916. There is no documented record of what his mistreatment may have been.

29 While at Montreaux, Cull wrote a letter to Ms Elizabeth Chomley, the Secretary of the Prisoner of War Department of the Australian Red Cross: 'The doctors here cannot understand why I was not repatriated direct to England. As far as is known at present the only thing they can do is to fit me up with irons. Mind you, Miss Chomley, I am not complaining. Pardon this scrawl for I am not over bright this evening.' AWMIDRL/0428, ARCS POW Dept, Capt. W. A. Cull.

30 AWM28, 'Recommendation files for honours and awards, AIF, 1914–18 War', File on Captain William Ambrose Cull, 22nd Battalion.

31 AWM27, 'Records arranged according to AWM Library subject classification', File 268/16, 'Regulations for

the War Office concerning awards to prisoners of war, March–May 1917', Memo dated 22 March 1917.

32   British War Office, *Army Orders* 1919, (London, HMSO, 1919), A.O.193.

33   'Albert Park By-Election', *The Argus*, 4 November 1919; 'Albert Park Election', *The Argus*, 11 November 1919; 'Salvation Army Appeal', *The Argus*, 15 November 1919; 'Repatriation: ANZAC Tweeds', *The Argus*, 28 November 1919.

34   Victorian BDM Marriage certificate, William Ambrose Cull and Doris Fenton Whitgelaw, 1920; National Archives of Australia, B2455 Personal Service Record, William Ambrose Cull, 'Officer's record of service'.

35   Victorian BDM Death certificate, William Ambrose Cull, August 1939; 'Fearless AIF officer—Collapse at party', *The Argus*, 31 July 1939; 'Obituary—Captain W. A. Cull', *The Argus*, 1 August 1939.